The Witch of Today

A Beginner's Guide to Potions, Herbs, Essential Oils, and More

Paige Cooper RN

Table of Contents

Introduction

The first image that pops into your head when you think about a witch inevitably has to be that of a hunchbacked old crone in dark robes peering at you from beneath the rim of a dusty pointed hat. She has a huge wart on her nose and another on her chin, and at least one of the warts has a long black hair growing out of it. If you have a vivid imagination, you also picture a mean-looking black cat peering at you from atop her shoulder. She could be the evil witch from any one of hundreds of children's stories such as Hansel and Gretel, Snow White and the Seven Dwarfs, or Sleeping Beauty.

In today's times, there are also many fantasy movies with witches in them, and more often than not, these witches are depicted as malicious evildoers with dark intentions and the powers to match, but what are witches really?

The Meaning of the Word 'Witch'

Most dictionaries describe a witch as a woman who is supposed to have supernatural powers. She practices black magic or sorcery with the aid of a familiar such as an animal or a devil. The word is also often used in a derogatory manner to describe a particularly unpleasant woman, and most of us have probably uttered the phrase, "she's a nasty old witch" at least once in our lives.

But this is not the true meaning of the word. In fact, it is very far from it. A witch is a person who is aligned with the natural energies of the universe. Such a person usually, but not always, practices some form of magick. They could be a healer, a seer, a card reader, a necromancer, a herbalist, someone who works with crystals, a psychic counselor, and so much more.

First of all, witches are not just female. The word 'witch' is gender-neutral and the majority of practitioners refer to themselves as such. The word 'mage' is sometimes used by witches who are deep into ceremonial magick and an older witch is sometimes called a sage or a crone. The misconception that a male witch is called a warlock was first created by the 1960's TV show, Bewitched, and was quickly picked up by the rest of Hollywood. In real life, however, a male witch would be insulted if you called him a warlock because it means 'oathbreaker' or 'deceiver.'

Magic or Magick?

The word 'magic' evokes images of the supernatural, the mysterious, the unexplained, and sometimes, the scary. It makes you think of folklore and fairytales, witches, wizards, and sorcerers. But it is also synonymous with the sleight of hand routines, card tricks, and illusions performed by stage and street magicians. Magic without a 'k' means so many things, and this is the main reason why many people prefer to use an alternative spelling of the word when they are referring to the magic of witchcraft and the occult world.

Magick with a 'k' was defined by the occultist, Aleister Crowley, as "the art or science of causing change to occur in conformity with Will." The late author, Scott Cunningham, defined it as "the projection of natural energies to produce needed effects," and Laurie Cabot, the well-known American witchcraft high priestess, defines it as follows: "Doing Magick allows an individual or group of individuals working in tandem, to align with the correct forces of the universe, the creator or the All."

To put it simply, magick means using the power of intention to make something happen that you want to happen. We will discuss this in deeper detail when we talk about spells later in the book.

The additional 'k' in the word 'magick' does not just differentiate it from performance magic and the magic of folklore and fairytales. Adding the letter 'k' has another significance which makes this spelling attractive to many practitioners.

The letter 'k' is the eleventh letter of several alphabets, and in numerology, the number eleven has a very high spiritual vibration. It carries a message of connection with our higher self. It is a channel for truth and inner wisdom. Many of the traits of its single-digit counterparts, the numbers two and one, also come through strongly, and the number is infused with innovativeness, creativity, harmony, empathy, and sensitivity to the needs of others. Magick brings with it the potential for great power, and the greater the power, the greater the responsibility that comes with it. The letter 'k' at the end of 'magick' is a signpost that points us on our way and constantly reminds us of this.

For the purpose of this book, we will be using the spelling, 'magick.'

Common Myths About Witches and Witchcraft

- **Real witches don't exist:** There is no way to prove to someone who refuses to believe that witches exist that they do. Such a person would insist on physical proof and maybe even ask the witch to perform some magic to prove that they are a witch. No self-respecting witch would even consider doing this and they might even be offended. All that is needed is that the witch knows that they exist, whether you believe in them or not.

- **Witches are evil:** This misconception has been created by movies, folklore, and fairytales. Yes, some witches are evil, but then, so are some other people who are not witches; so, being evil does not make you a witch, and being a witch does not make you evil.

- **You have to be Wiccan to be a witch:** Wicca is a religion that was founded in the 1950s by the anthropologist, Gerald Garner. The religion combines some of the traditions of witchcraft with modern elements and is loosely based on the Western European Pagan century-old rites and rituals that revere nature, observe the cycle of the seasons, and celebrate the harvest. Its practitioners are called Wiccans and you don't have to be one to be a witch. In fact, you don't have to follow any religion to be a witch or to practice witchcraft. It is simply because of the negative connotation of the word 'witch' that some practitioners of witchcraft incorrectly refer to themselves as Wiccans rather than calling themselves witches.

- **Witches sacrifice people and animals:** This is right up there with "Witches are evil" and while there are horror stories of witchdoctors and Voodoo practitioners that do terrible things to both animals and people, sacrificing animals and humans is definitely not part of being the kind of witch we are referring to. The witches we are referring to are the kind that respect nature and honor life, growth, beauty, and positive things.

- **You must be part of a coven to be a witch:** There is no need to join any kind of group to become a witch. We have already agreed that being a witch is recognizing your power and using it. You may need some skills, but you certainly do not need to join a group for that. However, joining a coven can be fun and interesting if you can find one. Witches, as a rule, do not advertise vacancies in their covens and you might want to rather start your own. Traditional covens have thirteen members and require witches to go through a strict initiation process before they may join. However, nowadays covens are much more casual and are often formed by groups of 'witchy' friends who practice magic together and share their ideas and knowledge.

- **You need special tools and loads of money to practice witchcraft:** All you need to practice witchcraft is *you*. While crystals, goblets, ceremonial daggers, crystal balls, tarot cards and other paraphernalia can be handy in rituals, they are not essential. Sharpen your craft with mediation and lots of reading on the subject, and look around you for your tools. The more you immerse yourself in your craft, the more you will notice that nature provides you with all you need. You can practice scrying by staring at the sky or at the water in a pond. The herbs you need might be growing in your garden or sitting on the spice rack in your kitchen. On your walk, you might just find the perfect stone or stick. The point is, you don't have to be rich to be a witch.

- **You have to worship a god or goddess to practice magic:** This misperception has been created by the Wiccan religion, but you really don't need to worship anything to practice magic. What you do need is respect for your environment, other people, and yourself, along with a strong sense of responsibility and a healthy dose of common sense.

Preparing you for your Journey

As you journey through this book, and if you are willing to open your mind, you will become more and more aware that you are a magical being and that the magick lives right there inside of you.

On your journey, you will learn about herbs and potions; you will learn about spells and how to create your own, and we will talk about one of the most important things that witches do—healing. But before we do that, we will talk a bit about the turbulent history of witches through the ages and we will inspect some of the rituals and beliefs of witchcraft. We'll also take a quick look at the witch of today—who they are, where to find them, and what they do and don't do.

Magick exists in many forms and it has been around since the beginning of time. If you can't see something, it doesn't mean that it doesn't exist—it just means you didn't know where to look. As you start practicing your own magick your eyes will open and you will start seeing the magick all around you. Remember to have fun and not take things too seriously. Let your journey begin!

Chapter 1: About Witches and Witchcraft

You have to know where you came from to know where you're going, and this is why we cannot just plunge into doing spells and making potions without understanding first what we are talking about and learning a little bit of the history surrounding witches and witchcraft.

The Definition of a Witch

To define something means to describe the exact nature of it. In order to describe the exact nature of something, you have to be able to put into words what it is. So how do we put into words what exactly a witch is?

If you look the word up in a dictionary, you will find that this is where the misperception starts that witches are evil females. The majority of descriptions automatically assume that a witch is a female person with magical or supernatural powers that she uses to either help or harm others. Some dictionaries assume that she is evil, wears a black cloak and a pointed hat and flies around on a broomstick.

If you go online and search using the words "what is a witch?" or "definition of a witch," you will not find a single website or article where that question is answered directly. The search results are dominated by links to various dictionaries that will define the word over and over but will not help you understand what a witch is.

That is because there is no answer to that question. A witch isn't a 'what.' A witch is a 'who.' A witch isn't a *thing* with certain characteristics and abilities that can be described in a short sentence or even in a long article. Each witch is a unique, magical individual with their own skills, beliefs, ideas, and talents.

Witches come from all walks of life and just because someone doesn't call themselves a witch doesn't mean they aren't one. A witch is simply a person who is attuned to the energies of the universe and knows how to use their inner power to attract their wants and desires. They acknowledge and use their psychic talents and healing abilities and usually have a close connection with nature.

A witch could be someone who actively practices magick by doing rituals and spells, or it could be a psychic medium or a tarot reader; it could even be the lady on the corner who reads tea leaves and uses herbs and essential oils to make potions. Shamans, Reiki practitioners and animal whisperers can also be considered witches. In fact, any person who taps into the power of the universe for the purpose of bringing about some or other kind of change might be considered a witch by today's standards. There are kitchen witches, country witches, herbalist witches, city witches, cottage witches, crystal witches, seer witches, healer witches and even influencer witches! In fact, you can be any kind of witch that you want to be. If you cast spells by drawing pictures and you want to call yourself a crayon witch, you are free to do so. There are no restrictions on what kind of witch you can be.

Some witches practice their craft for themselves and others do it to earn their income. Online shops and physical shops where you can buy all sorts of 'witchy' paraphernalia from wands and candles and cauldrons to lotions, positions and crystals have been popping up like mushrooms on the internet and on the streets. Witches who are shamans and Reiki practitioners might offer their services as healers. Others will do tarot or other psychic readings and some will perform rituals or cast spells for you.

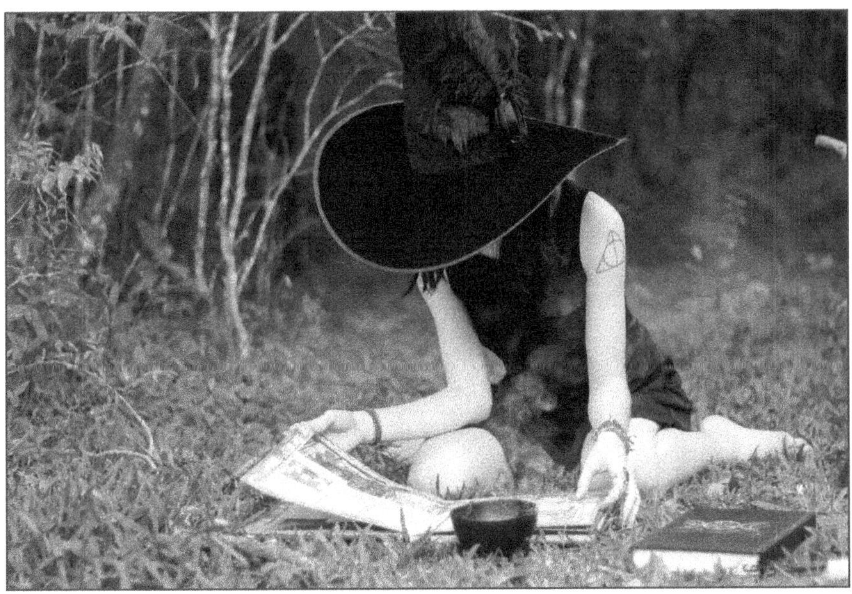

Are You a Witch?

By now you know a little bit more about witches. You have a basic idea of who they are, what they do, and what characteristics they have. We've agreed that the one thing that all witches have in common, is that they are attuned to the energies of the universe. But what exactly does this mean? How do you know if you're attuned to the energies of the universe?

Here are some examples of what it means to be attuned to the energies of the universe. As you go through them, see which ones apply to you, if any.

- You feel "at one" with nature when you're outside. You give in to the urge to kick off your shoes so that you can stand barefoot on the earth and "soak up" some energy whenever you can.

- Your spirit is stirred by the sight and sound of thunder and lightning, heavy winds, giant waves, and other natural events. Because witches are in tune with the natural energy of the earth, these events are a perfect opportunity to recharge.

- You have a strong sense of intuition, or, as it is sometimes called, a sixth sense. For instance, someone is telling you something, and you instinctively know that they are lying, or you meet a new person and you immediately have a good or bad feeling about them. More often than not, when you think about someone, not long after, they call you or you run into them somewhere. You probably go by what is called your "gut feeling" when you make decisions and choices.

- Animals are drawn to you and you to them; whether they are domestic animals or wildlife makes no difference. Because witches are in tune with nature, they have the kind of energy that animals are attracted to. Your pets probably respond when you call them by name, and you have 'conversations' with them.

- You're always collecting precious stones, gems, trinkets, bones, shells, feathers, little pieces of wood, and all sorts of things that attract your attention. You keep them in a box or display them in your garden and in your home. Once you've finished this book, take a look at them again, and you will realize that you've been collecting the 'tools' of your craft.

- You have a fascination with herbs, and in particular, the ones that have healing capabilities. You have a knack for growing them and working with them.

- You feel drawn by the energy of a full moon—this is a strong indication that you're a witch. Some witches may even feel different energies during the different phases of the moon.

- You notice the presence of symbols that pop up regularly in your daily life and you're able to interpret them. For example, you've been noticing a lot of white feathers lately, and also that every time just after seeing the white feather, you see yellow daisies. You instinctively know that this is your late Aunt Daisy saying hello from the other side. Or, you might even be able to interpret messages that tell you something about the future, or what to avoid. You are practicing a form of divination and this is a sure sign that you're a witch.

- You have the ability to make others feel better simply by being around them and listening to them. This makes you a healer, and healers are witches.

- You have an avid interest in the esoteric and you might own a book or two on the subject. You've done some research online and you've watched a couple of videos. You might even own a tarot deck and have several crystals on your shelf. Maybe you meditate regularly, or at least once in a while.

If some of these traits apply to you, you are a witch whether you want to know it or not. You might not feel comfortable with calling yourself a witch, but that doesn't mean that you aren't one.

No matter what you call the sun, or whether you call it nothing at all, it will still have the characteristics of the sun. It comes up every morning and goes down every evening and warms us with its light as it crosses the sky on its daily journey. You can call it the moon, or nothing at all, but it will still be the sun and it will still do what the sun does.

In the same way, whether you call yourself a witch, or an esoteric, or nothing at all, if you have the characteristics and talents of a witch, that's what you are. Being a witch isn't like being an architect or a shop assistant or a doctor or a lawyer. You don't suddenly turn into a witch when you actively begin practicing witchcraft. You're already a witch—you are just an unskilled one. A witch is something that you are because of your nature, talents, and characteristics; it is not something you become after you've studied or trained for it. However, you can study and train to become a practicing witch, and of course, most witches constantly study to improve their skills.

Witchcraft

The Merriam-Webster dictionary defines witchcraft as "the use of sorcery or magic" and "communication with the devil or with a familiar." The Oxford Advanced Learner's Dictionary states that witchcraft is "the use of magic powers, especially evil ones," and the Cambridge Dictionary simply says that witchcraft is "the use of magic, especially in stories, to help or harm people." If you dig a bit deeper, you will find sources that state that witchcraft is communion with the devil, ancestors, and deities.

These definitions are outdated and derogatory. They create a bad impression of witches and witchcraft, and practitioners have gone as far as raising petitions insisting that these descriptions be updated to reflect the meaning of witchcraft in today's world. Thus far none of these petitions appear to have been successful and these definitions continue to appear in dictionaries.

Modern witchcraft is almost as hard to define as the witches who practice it, and this could be one of the reasons why the writers of dictionaries have not updated it yet. Rather than simply call it "witchcraft," we shall speak about "modern witchcraft." This will help us to differentiate between traditional witchcraft as described in dictionaries, and the craft that modern witches practice today.

So how do we define modern witchcraft? Witchcraft is first and foremost the craft practiced by witches—that much is obvious. We've managed to define the modern witch as a person who is attuned with the energies of the universe, so now we need to figure out what the 'craft' part of the word means. This is much less complicated than it seems. The craft is everything you do as a witch. It's casting spells, reading the tarot, palmistry, scrying, communicating with animals, growing herbs, creating potions, healing, and anything else that you do with the intention of bringing about positive change. The best way to define modern witchcraft for our purposes would therefore be to say that witchcraft means employing the energies of the universe to bring about positive change.

Where Do the Misperceptions About Witchcraft Come From?

Especially in the West, witchcraft was traditionally seen as a craft that was practiced in darkness by evil witches who had pacts with demons and devils, took part in dark rites, and called on supernatural powers to control events and people. This is not witchcraft. This kind of practice is called sorcery. Sorcery is dark or black magic and its intent is always to cause harm to others.

People have believed in witchcraft since the existence of mankind. They paid tribute to gods and goddesses and believed that they brought rains and good crops. There were gods for the seasons and the weather, and for almost anything else you can think of. During bad times when the rains stayed away or the winter was particularly harsh, witches, shamans, and medicine people were called upon to cast spells and perform rituals to "speak to the gods." Ironically, even though these practitioners were mostly wise healers, they were seen as beings with supernatural powers who had the ability to either nurture or destroy, and over time, people came to fear them.

In the 15th century the Black Plague raged across Europe and a series of natural disasters caused further devastation. Because witches were healers and guardians of the seasons and weather they were the obvious culprits and people blamed them for what was happening. Everybody agreed that they had to be punished for their 'evildoing' and this was the beginning of the persecution of witches.

Witch Spotting

For the next few centuries, witch spotting became somewhat of a national sport in many countries. Those who were suspected of witchcraft were subjected to some of the most bizarre and cruel tests imaginable or simply tortured until they confessed.

Below are some of the methods that were used to identify witches:

- Thumbscrews: During the time of the Holy Roman Empire, the judges used thumbscrews that were tightened until the person confessed that they were a witch.
- The 'swimming' test: This was a popular folk method whereby witches were bound and thrown into the nearest body of water to see if they would sink or float. If they floated, they were a witch. If they sank to the bottom, they were innocent and were hauled out and set free if they hadn't already drowned. It was believed that witches spurned the sacrament of baptism, and therefore, the water would reject them and they would float.
- Public examination: The suspect was stripped naked, shaved from head to foot and then publicly examined to see if they had the Devil's mark or a witch's teat.

  According to the beliefs of the time, Satan branded his followers, and these marks were called the Devil's mark. Depending on the examiner, and sometimes the mood of the crowd, the Devil's mark could be anything from a mole to a birthmark to a scar or even just a red spot from an insect bite. It was believed that the Devil would not allow one of his own to be harmed, so a long silver pin was used to prick any suspicious marks. If there was no blood or the suspect didn't react, they were a witch.

  It was believed that witches had a third nipple to suckle demons, and again, this could be anything from a real third nipple (which is actually quite common) to a wart or even a mole.

Some people were so terrified that they would try to remove any marks that could have them mistaken for a witch by cutting or even burning them off. Unfortunately, this just made things worse and they were accused of trying to remove evidence which was considered sufficient proof of their covenant with the Devil.

- The ducking stool: This was a device similar to a seesaw that was placed at the edge of a body of water. One end of the seesaw was on land and the other hung over the water. The end over land had a rope attached for pulling on, and the other end had a chair of some sort attached to it. The suspect was tied to the chair and dunked under the water until they either drowned or confessed.

- Pressing: The suspect was laid on a board with another board over them. Accusers would then stack heavy rocks on it until the suspect confessed or the weight of the rocks crushed them to death.

- Scratching: The supposed victim of the witch would scratch them with their fingernails. If the victim felt relief or improvement and the scratches drew blood, it was proof that the accused was a witch.

- The prayer test: Accused witches were made to recite the Lord's Prayer from the Bible without making a single mistake. Stuttering, mispronunciation, or even signs of nervousness were considered proof of their being a witch. When they did manage to recite the prayer flawlessly, it was said that the accused had been assisted by the devil and they were executed anyway.

These are just a few of the means by which witches were 'identified' in Medieval times. There were many other ways, each one with the potential to be more bizarre than the next. Interestingly enough, as bizarre and unfair as these tests were, more than fifty percent of the surviving accused were declared innocent.

The Execution of Witches

Punishment for being a witch was always the death sentence—it was the means of execution that differed. Contrary to popular belief, burning at the stake only happened in European countries where the law stated that malevolent witchcraft should be punished by fire. In England and its American colonies witchcraft was considered a felony and was punished by hanging, while in Scotland, the guilty were strangled to death before their bodies were burned. In some other countries, beheading was the punishment of choice. In all cases, no matter the style of execution, it was made sure that the bodies were burned to ashes to ensure that the witch could not practice their sorcery from beyond the grave.

The Salem Witch Trials

You can't talk about witchcraft and the execution of witches and leave out the famous Salem Witch Trials. These trials have been the inspiration of many Hollywood movies and fantasy novels and this has resulted

in there being loads of misperceptions about what really happened. Many people imagine massive witch-burnings and all sorts of terrible things. While it wasn't pleasant, it wasn't all that the movies and story-tellers make of it. Here's what really happened.

One day in January 1692, in the town of Salem, Massachusetts, out of the blue, two young girls started displaying extremely strange behavior. They were having violent convulsions and screaming as if they were being tortured. A physician examined them and diagnosed that they had been bewitched.

This led to mass hysteria in the little village. Over the next nine months more than one hundred people were accused of being witches and put in jail. Nineteen women were found guilty and hung. The only man who had been accused refused to confess to anything and was pressed to death with heavy stones as described above. Many of the accused died while they were incarcerated. Contrary to popular belief, not a single witch was burned at the stake in Salem.

And what was really the matter with the two girls who started it all? Nobody really knows. Some theorize that the convulsions are an indication that they were suffering from clinical hysteria and others say they were just good actresses.

Why Practice Modern Witchcraft?

Why would you want to practice modern witchcraft? What do you use it for? What are the benefits? These are questions that people ask on a regular basis, and the answers you get would depend on whom you are asking. The herbalist might say that they want to create potions to heal people. The animal whisperer tells you that they have a deep desire to help people understand their pets better. The witch who casts spells for you says they do it because they care about other people's happiness. The healer is concerned with repairing the mind, body and spirit. The psychic who reads the tarot uses their abilities to guide and help people make more informed decisions. All these people have one thing in common—they are acting on their desire to bring about positive change through practicing their craft.

Modern witchcraft isn't about religion; it is about spirituality. Many modern witches choose their path because they have a need to explore their spirituality outside of the strictures of organized religion. There are no gods that have to be worshipped; there are no fixed rules and rituals, and the only person you have to answer to is yourself. This isn't as easy and happy-go-lucky as it sounds. The reason why no gods, rules, or rituals are needed, is that the modern witch takes responsibility for their own actions and the results that come from them.

Ethics of Modern Witchcraft

With great power comes even greater responsibility; the deeper you get into your personal craft, the stronger your power will grow, and the stronger your power is, the more aware you have to be of how you use it. Because magick is performed through attunement with the energies of the universe, everything you do affects everything else.

To help you understand this better, let's imagine a huge spider web that is hanging between two trees. The spider web represents the universe; everything is connected to everything else by a single thread. You take a twig and ever so gently poke at the web. This action represents you sending your intention into the universe to manifest a desire. You will notice that not just the part where you touched the web moves—the whole thing vibrates. In the same way, if you perform magick, it doesn't just affect you or the person you are doing it for. It causes a vibration that affects the entire universe.

Magick and the Universal Laws

Just like there are laws in physics, such as Newton's universal law of gravitation and Ohms law of current, there are also universal laws. While the laws of physics have to do with the physical, the universal laws are about the energies of the universe and will therefore also apply to magick. Whether you believe in them or not, and whether you understand them or not, they are always working and they apply to you and everything else in the universe.

These laws are based on the knowledge that everything in the universe is energy, and because of this, everything is connected. Everything is part of everything else in some way or another. You can picture the spider web in the example above, or, let's try another way: Think of the universe as a huge pot of vegetable soup. The liquid part of the soup represents all the space between things, like the air and the sky and the clouds—everything that you are aware of but cannot see or touch. The vegetables, noodles and whatever else is in the soup represent everything that is tangible; the planet, people, buildings, cars, even water—anything that has any kind of substance. So whether you can see it or not, it is all still part of one great big pot of soup. No matter where you insert a spoon, it doesn't just affect the part of the soup where you inserted the spoon. No matter how carefully you do it, all the soup will move, even if it's just slightly. If one part of the soup is affected, the entire pot of soup is affected.

There are essentially seven laws or principles by which the universe is governed. Teachings dating back more than 5,000 years all have these seven laws as a common thread. If you make the effort to understand these laws, align yourself with them, and apply them in your daily life and in your magical practice you will experience your inner power beyond anything you ever could imagine. These ancient laws are what make modern magick work.

The first three of the seven laws are called immutable laws. They have existed since the beginning of time and will cease to exist only if time itself ceases to exist. These laws can never be changed or transcended. The remaining four laws are called mutable laws. These are laws that can be transcended, meaning that you can rise above them and use them to your advantage.

Let's take a look at the seven universal laws:

1. The Law of Mentalism: There is a single, intelligent consciousness from which all things manifest. It has many names, one of which is the Universal Mind. Your mind is part of this Universal Mind and therefore also has the power to manifest, which is why we say that it is your own thoughts and intentions that create your reality. Very simply put, this law says that for anything to exist in the physical world, it has to exist in the mind first.

2. The Law of Correspondence: This law says that everything in the universe, you included, originates from a single source. The phrase, "as above, so below; as below, so above" is often used when casting a spell. What it means is that there is no separation between the physical, spiritual, and mental realms. They are in correspondence, harmony and agreement with each other.

3. The Law of Vibration: This is the last of the three immutable laws. It simply tells us that everything is constantly in a state of vibration. Science has confirmed that everything in the entire universe, including you, is pure energy that is vibrating on different frequencies. Your thoughts and emotions are also vibrations, and these can be controlled by you. The vibration for unconditional love is the highest of the emotional vibrations. The energy for hate on the other hand, is dark, dense and base. Focusing on positive thoughts and emotions will help you raise our vibration. The higher you can raise your vibration, the more in tune you become with the pure energies of the universe.

4. The Law of Polarity: This is the first of the mutable laws. It tells us that everything has an opposite and that opposites are actually just two extremes of the same thing. For example, hot and cold are both degrees of temperature. Cold is low and hot is high, but it is still just varying degrees of temperature that we're talking about. Similarly, love and hate are varying degrees of affection; sadness is a low degree of joy, and so on. Positive emotions have higher vibrations than negative emotions, and the same goes for positive thoughts and actions. You can transcend the Law of Polarity by raising your vibration, and you do this by persistently focusing on the positive or the good, even when things are not so good.

5. The Law of Rhythm: This law states that everything is like a pendulum. Tides come in and go out, seasons come and go, empires rise and fall, businesses start up and close down, and even in your own life you will notice that you have hard

times and times when things are going well. This law only operates in the physical and mental realms; not in the spiritual realm. You can transcend it if you remember who you are—that your mind is part of the Universal Mind. Find the good in everything and keep focusing on the positive and you will raise your vibration to a point where you can transcend this law.

6. The Law of Cause and Effect: This law says: "Every cause has its effect; every effect has its cause." Everything you say, do, and think, sets something in motion in the universe that will eventually materialize in some or other form. The stronger the intent with which the words, thoughts, or actions are repeated, the stronger the vibration they will create in the universe. That is why spells and prayers work. When you say something with intent, it immediately manifests in the spiritual realm. Our concept of time and space causes a time lag between the spiritual manifestation and the physical event. The stronger you can visualize and imagine the physical event, the sooner and more likely it is to manifest.

7. The Law of Gender: This law tells us that everyone and everything has both masculine and feminine elements. Some of the outward expressions of the masculine elements are energy, intellect, self-reliance, and logic. These warm energies are balanced by the cooling female energies of patience, love, intuition, gentleness, kindness, and such. Within each of us lie the latent qualities of both the male and the female. When you acknowledge this and accept it, you will know what it is to feel complete.

The Law of Attraction

You may have been wondering why the Law of Attraction wasn't included in the list above. The Law of Attraction isn't counted as one of the seven laws because it is the law that encompasses all the other universal laws. It is the basic law upon which all the other laws rest and the fabric that holds it all together. If you understand the law of attraction, your understanding of the other laws will come naturally. You will also understand how magick works.

The Law of Attraction will help you when you focus your intention on that which you desire to manifest. In accordance with this law, you attract into your life the things and circumstances that dominate your thoughts and beliefs, both consciously and subconsciously. For example, if you have a belief that money is scarce, you will find that you always feel that you have a shortage of it.

You will remember that we said that each of your thoughts, actions, and intentions create a vibration in the universe. Each of these vibrations has its own frequency that corresponds with the vibration of what you will attract. If you wish for happiness but you are constantly focused on your misfortune, you will keep on attracting more and more misfortune into your life. To attract happiness, you have to focus on the positive things in your life. If you want to lose weight, you must not think about losing weight, because then you're focusing on the weight. You must think about what you will gain. Think about the advantages of your healthy diet and lifestyle. Focus on the end result, not on what you want to leave behind.

Chapter 2: The Tools of the Craft

Herbs

Herbs, healing, and witchcraft have been associated with each other since the beginning of time, and considering that plants inhabited the planet long before human beings even evolved, it could be said that herbs are the oldest magical tool that exists. Herbs have always been known for their healing properties, both physical and spiritual, and these plants have been used, and are still used by healers, shamans, witches, and other practitioners of natural medicine. And of course, they are also used in spells.

Herbal Lore

Herbal medicine is as ancient as the practice of witchcraft and its use derives from the need of mankind to cure ailments, mend wounds, and promote both physical and mental health. Many of the medicines of today have been developed from these herbal cures. Some are still used in parts of the world in their natural form, but, especially in Western countries they have been discarded for supposedly stronger, more effective synthetic drugs, and many doctors scoff at these herbal cures. However, in recent times, herbal remedies have become more popular and particularly the properties of foxglove have been noted as a remedy for heart disease. Witches have known this for ages.

Healing powers have been attributed to a wide variety of plants since the beginning of time, and the witches of the past had great knowledge of these herbs, plants, and flowers. As a natural healer, a witch should have a good knowledge of human anatomy, but they are also required to be a psychologist and counselor. Many illnesses are caused by psychological issues, and sometimes the most important part of the cure is understanding the psychological issue behind the illness. Because they are connected and aligned with the energies of the universe, many witches are able to pick up the vibrations of their patient and this enables them to instinctively 'know' what it is that the patient needs to enable and speed up their healing.

According to magical symbolism, the four elements required to sustain life are Earth, Water, Fire and Air. Plants embody the power of all four of these elements. The plant begins its life as a seed in the soil of the earth where it is fed and sustained by the minerals in the ground. Of course, water is required for any plant to grow—even the hardiest cactus needs the odd drop of moisture occasionally. Fire represents the sunlight that is captured by the leaves of plants to assist with the conversion of carbon dioxide, water and minerals into oxygen and other energy-rich compounds. The release of oxygen into the atmosphere affects the air and makes it suitable for humans and animals to breathe. The air is the wind that blows and stimulates the growth of stems and leaves and makes them stronger. It is also the wind that picks up the seed and drops it somewhere miles away where it will germinate and grow to continue the cycle of life.

How to Get the Most Out of Herbs

When you decide to go out collecting herbs, it is a good idea to decide on just one or two at a time. It is important to find the best time of the day to collect them. Some herbs are best picked in the early morning, others around noon, and others should be collected in the evening or even at night. When picking your herbs, only take the parts that you need. If it's just the leaves you need, then don't break off the stem as well. This ensures that you don't stunt the growth of future crops.

Many plants have similarities that can confuse you, so you should be very careful when choosing your herbs to make sure that they are what you think they are. There is no limit on the number of books, illustrations, and examples that you can study to learn how to recognize these important tools of your craft. If you can learn to refer to herbs and plants by their Latin names, this will stand you in good stead as these names never change. The common names for plants and herbs differ from region to region and some have up to twenty names that will just add to your confusion.

While herbs and plants can heal, they can also harm, and this is one of the main reasons why you should make a point of studying your subject and learning as much as you can. Some herbs or plants can be lethal if used incorrectly or at all. Mandrake or Mayapple, poison hemlock, skunk cabbage, and castor oil seeds are the most dangerous and should never be ingested. You should make sure that you know what they look like so that you do not mistake them for something else. Other plants that can make you sick if they are ingested or could cause allergic reactions include passion flowers, coltsfoot, comfrey root and leaves, lobelia, wild cherries, bogbean, juniper berries, peppermint, thyme, wild carrot, fennel, hops, wild indigo, and yarrow. This is not a comprehensive list, and before you use any herb or plant, it is important to first make sure that you know all of its properties and what it is used for.

Collecting and working with herbs

Treat your herbs with care when you pick them. Collect them in small bundles to make sure that you don't crush or damage them. Your poultices and decoctions can sometimes be spoiled or wasted simply because you didn't prepare your herbs or plants correctly. Do not let this discourage you. It's a learning process, and you will get better at it as you go along. Herbs are also usually mild in action and it may take time to show results, and this might make you think that it is not working.

To derive the natural benefits from herbs and plants, they have to be prepared and used in specific ways. Decoction and infusion for instance, produce different results from the same plant. Decoction extracts the resinous, bitter principles of the plant while infusion releases and extracts the aromatic essences. Decoction and infusion are not the only ways to treat herbs; the other processes are called comminution, extraction, percolation, filtration, clarification, digestion, and expression. Let's take a look at these processes:

- **Comminution**

  Comminution means the reduction of materials from their original size to a smaller size by means of crushing, grinding, cutting, or vibration. In simple terms, it means reducing your herbs to smaller particles so that you can dry them and store them. While there are machines available for cutting and milling of herbs, the pestle and mortar remains a favorite among practitioners of magick for this purpose.

  All herbs that you intend to store should be completely free from moisture so that they do not mold or mildew. Some herbs must not be dried at high temperatures, and others must not dry too slowly. They must not get moisture during the drying process, or they will mildew. This is not as complicated as it sounds and with the guidelines provided below, you will have no problems with preparing your herbs for storage.

☐ Collect your herbs that you are going to prepare for storage on a dry day.

☐ Tie your herbs with thread in twos so that the bundles are joined together by the piece of thread. Hang by the thread from your clothesline or any other place outside where it is warm, dry, and sunny. At night, or if the weather gets damp, you need to move them indoors to a dry space otherwise they will mildew.

☐ If you collected only leaves and flowers, these should be put in a muslin bag to dry and can also be hung outside. Be careful to not put too many in the bag or the air will not be able to move through and they will not dry properly.

☐ Move your bundles and bags around so that they get as much sun as possible. If there is very little sun and you need to dry your herbs indoors, the best temperature to keep them at is between 65° and 70° F.

☐ When your bundles are dry, you can first pass them through a meat grinder if you have one, or you can chop them up in your blender and crush them further with a mortar and pestle. If you've dried them properly, they should come out almost in powder form. You can store them in cans or bottles with tops or corks that seal well. Keep them in the dark, and they will last for several years without losing their medicinal properties or natural color.

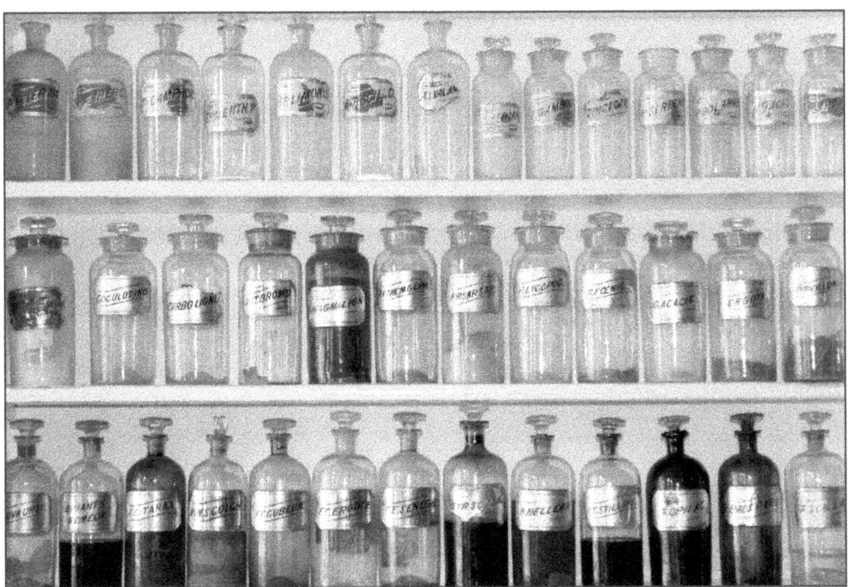

- **Extraction**

Extraction is the process of selectively removing a compound from something using some sort of solvent such as water or alcohol. Making tea is a good example of this process. The essence of tea leaves is extracted by pouring boiling water on them, and the resulting liquid is the extract. Three methods of extraction are used when working with herbs. These are decoction, infusion, and maceration.

  - **Decoction** is the process of creating a preparation by boiling herbs in a liquid, usually water. The end product is also called a decoction and it has many purposes. An herbal decoction can be enjoyed as a strong herbal drink or be used as the base for herbal syrups or poultices.

How to make a decoction: Add about a tablespoon of herbs for every cup of cold water to a pot and bring it up to a gentle boil. Cover the pot with a lid and let it simmer for twenty to forty minutes, depending on the number of herbs and water you have in your pot. Let it stand to cool down to drinking temperature, and finish it up by straining out the herbs. Sometimes you can re-use the herbs to make further decoctions, depending on how strong you made the first lot.

The list of what you can use for decoctions is endless, so it is better to simply say that it is best for extracting the essence of hard or woody plants, and parts of plants such as roots, bark, seeds, nuts, berries, or mushrooms.

A few tips for a successful decoction:

- ☐ Always use cold water.

- ☐ If you're using fresh herbs, you should use more of them since they have a higher water content than dried herbs.

- ☐ Crush or grind fresh, and even powdered, herbs before you brew them. It increases the surface area of the herb and more of its essence can be extracted.

- ☐ You can infuse your decoction by combining it with herbs that work best for infusions. First you decoct your hard, woody herbs, and once you remove it from the heat, you add the remaining herbs. Keep the pot covered while it stands so that all the herbs can infuse together.

- *Infusion* is the process of obtaining extracts from herbs and plants by steeping them in hot, but not boiling water. In some cases you will even use cold water. This method makes it easy to extract the flavors and oils from herbs and plants for drinking purposes, whether it's for the taste, or for the medicinal value.

  Making herbal tea is a form of infusion because it's made by steeping the leaves in hot water. However, because the steeping time is so short, the resulting drink is rather weak. For true infusions where you want a strong end result, roots, shoots, leaves, and flowers of plants are typically used and steeped for a much longer time. This is sometimes called a "long infusion."

  Infusions are popular with health enthusiasts who don't like taking pills, since they are a more natural way of taking herbs. Others simply drink it for the taste.

- *Maceration* means the breaking down or softening of something by soaking it in a liquid such as water, oil, or alcohol for a variable period. To macerate your herbs, simply put them in a container and cover them with the chosen liquid. Gently stir the mixture to release any trapped air bubbles before capping the jar securely. Keep it in a warm place and shake it daily. It takes about four weeks for your infusion to be ready, after which, you can just strain the liquid and pour it into clean bottles for later use.

- ## Percolation

Percolation is one of the best methods to make liquid extracts from herbal material. It is similar to maceration, so if you do not have, or cannot get hold of the equipment for percolation, maceration will serve your purpose just as well. Percolation simply means that you're dripping alcohol or water very slowly through powdered herbs that have been packed into a cone. The solvent drips out of the herb through a filtered bottom into a container where it is collected.

The main advantage of this method is that it is very fast. It takes only one or two days before you have the final product. The downside is that you need specialized equipment that you will either have to make or buy, and you can only use dried herbs.

- ## Filtration

Filtration is simply the process of separating liquids from solids by using muscle power to squeeze out the liquid. The most popular way to do this is to put a piece of cheesecloth over a bowl and then pour whatever you wish to filter into the cloth. Now you simply gather the corners and edges in such a way that nothing can spill out, fasten it, and squeeze the contents as hard as you can. The solid matter will stay behind in the cloth, and the liquid will end up in the bowl.

- **Clarification**

  Clarification usually applies to substances such as honey, syrups, lard, and so on. It is done by skimming or melting or filtering the substance through a suitable material to remove any particles and make it clear.

- **Digestion**

  Digestion is prolonged maceration at a constant temperature of 100°F.

- **Expression**

  Expression means to extract the juices from herbs by squeezing it out by using a press. A simple screw press can be used, and there are also large hydraulic presses that are used in laboratories.

Now that you know how to pick and process and store your herbs, it is time to find out how to use them.

Making Herb Simples

A 'simple' is when you use only one herb at a time. Many people prefer using 'simples' because each herb has a specific way of acting, and when they are combined, it is not possible to take note of the individual actions of each herb.

Simples are easy to make. For finely ground or chopped herbs, you can steep a heaped teaspoonful per cup in hot, but not boiling water for about 20 minutes. Flowers and leaves are also steeped in hot water, but they should be covered so that the oil doesn't evaporate. Powdered herbs can be taken with hot or cold water by simply mixing a teaspoonful into a cup of water and drinking it down. This should always be followed by a glass of plain water. Roots and bark should be simmered gently for at least half an hour, and preferably longer, to get all the goodness out of them. It is very important to remember to never use aluminum pots to boil herbs or water as the metal damages the fine oils in the herbs.

Making Syrups

The purpose of syrups is simply to enhance the taste of some herbs which can be quite bitter and nasty. To make your syrup, all you need to do, is to boil a pint of water and three pounds of brown sugar until it is thick. If you want to make herb syrup, simply add the cut herbs as well. When it is ready, strain it through cheesecloth to remove the herbs and bottle. If your bottles are corked, or sealed airtight, your syrups can last indefinitely. Malt and honey from bees can also be used as syrups.

Making Herb Ointments

To make a basic ointment, you will need vegetable fat, cocoa fat, or lard; beeswax, and the herbs of your choice. These should preferably be fresh, but dried herbs will also do. For every eight ounces of lard, you need two ounces of beeswax. Your herbs should be chopped very finely or crushed. How much you add depends on which herb or herbs you are using. Simmer the herbs with the lard or fat of your choice in the top of a double boiler for several hours. When the fat is properly infused with the herbs, strain it to get the pieces out and put the pot back on the stove. Melt the beeswax into it and when all the wax is melted in, pour it into a jar for storage. Remember to heat up the jar by immersing it in hot water and then drying it properly before adding your ointment. If you don't heat up the jar, the heat of the mixture is likely to cause it to crack.

Making Poultices

Poultices are simply a paste made from crushed herbs or leaves. This is applied directly to the skin on the affected area. Poultices are great for superficial burns, rashes, bruises, cuts, and other skin ailments as well as swelling and enlarged glands. Poultices can also be applied on the skin area over an internal organ to relieve pain or draw out toxins. Once a poultice has been removed, it should be thrown away. It should never be reused.

To get you started, here are some poultices that you can safely use:

- *Lobelia and slippery elm*—excellent for cold sores, abscesses, ulcers, boils, blood poisoning, and even pain and inflammation of the joints. Use one third part lobelia and two thirds slippery elm to make your poultice.

- *Charcoal and smartweed*—relieves inflammation of the bowels, and if it's used to treat cold sores or ulcers, add one or all three of the following: myrrh, goldenseal, and Echinacea.

- *Sage*—relieves all types of inflammation.

- *Hyssop*—removes the discoloration from bruises. Apply the poultice as hot as possible and replace it with a new one as soon as the heat dissipates.
- *Plantain*—use to treat small wounds and cuts, inflamed skin, eczema, insect bites and stings. Bruise or crush the leaves and apply them directly on the skin.
- *Chickweed*—the leaves can be used to treat itching, muscle and joint pain, and a skin disease called psoriasis.
- *Calendula*—reduces pain and swelling due to inflammation and is also good for treating leg ulcers and poorly healing wounds.
- *Dandelion leaves*—great for treating skin conditions such as acne and eczema.
- *Burdock root*—you can treat gout, joint pain, acne, psoriasis and a variety of other skin conditions with a burdock root poultice.

Crystals

You probably don't really need crystals in your witch's toolbox, but why go without them? Crystals are a beautiful addition, and the more you understand about them, the more value you will find in them. Not all crystals are expensive, and there are many shops where you can find wonderful crystals at affordable prices. Some people will tell you that they didn't choose the crystals that they own. The crystals chose them.

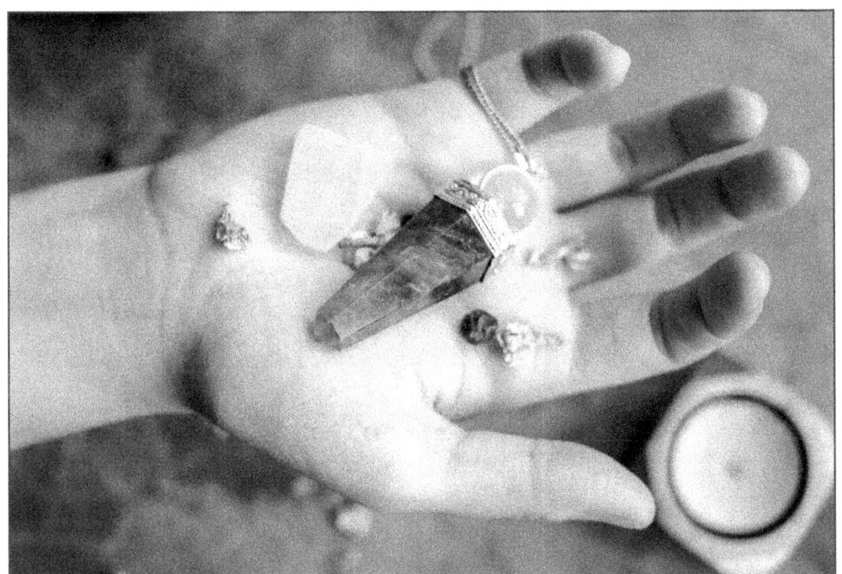

You may be in a shop and a specific crystal will catch your eye, or you may even get an urge to rummage in a box or look at a specific shelf, and suddenly you come across a crystal that you know just *has* to come home with you!

Crystals can be used for a multitude of purposes including healing, scrying, casting spells, balancing energies, cleansing, dispelling negative energy, enhancing the properties of other elements, and making elixirs.

It would be impossible to list all the crystals that are available along with their properties in this book, so, to get you going, we will look at ten crystals that are relatively easy to get hold of and are popularly used by witches.

- **Clear Quartz:** If this is the only crystal you ever own, it will still be enough. Clear Quartz is the most versatile of all the crystals and can be used for almost anything. Its unique helical spiral crystalline form makes it the most powerful energy and healing amplifier on the planet. Clear Quartz can also be used for any ailment or condition because it stimulates the immune system and restores balance in the body. It contains every possible color in the spectrum and works on all levels of being. Spiritually, it raises energy to the highest possible level and stores information like a natural computer. It can be used to filter out distractions during meditation; it boosts the powers of other crystals and even herbs, and it can be used to dispel negative energy. Quartz comes in a variety of colors, and each color stone has the intrinsic properties of clear quartz along with its own additional properties.

- **Amethyst:** This is one of the most common crystals, but also one of the most powerful because of its high spiritual vibration. It comes in various shades of purple and is most often found in clusters or geode form. Amethyst provides extremely powerful protection, enhances spiritual awareness, and has strong cleansing and healing powers. It is highly beneficial to the mind—it will calm and stimulate as required and help you stay focused and in control of your facilities. It enhances memory and improves motivation, promotes emotional centering by balancing out highs and lows, and brings common sense and spiritual insights.

  When used for healing, Amethyst tunes the endocrine system and boosts the productions of hormones. It cleanses the blood and relieves physical, emotional, and psychological pain and stress. It eases headaches by releasing the tension that causes them, and it can reduce bruises and swellings. It can also be used to treat hearing disorders, respiratory diseases, skin conditions, and problems with the digestive tract.

- **Rose Quartz:** As the name suggests, Rose Quartz is a beautiful, translucent pink color. It is quite common and easy to get hold of, and you will find it in its rough form or tumbled and polished to a glossy shine. This crystal speaks to the heart chakra. It is the stone of unconditional love and infinite peace and purifies and opens the heart, bringing inner healing and self-love. Romantic Rose Quartz is perfect for attracting love into your life and is a popular component in love spells.

  As a healing stone, it strengthens the heart and circulatory system. It can be placed on the thymus for chest and lung problems. It alleviates vertigo and heals the kidneys and adrenals. It is also said to increase fertility and it is beneficial for patients with Alzheimer's, Parkinson's, and senile dementia.

- **Jasper:** Jasper comes in a wide variety of colors and is easy to find. Jasper stones are nurturing stones. They bring tranquility and provide support during stress. Jasper can be used in chakra layouts to align the chakras; it is grounding and balances yin and yang, and aligns the emotional, mental, and physical bodies with the etheric realm.

  As a healing stone, Jasper balances the mineral content of the body and supports the digestive, circulatory, and reproductive organs. It is especially useful as an elixir for calming and other purposes because it doesn't overstimulate the body. Jasper is also said to prolong and enhance sexual pleasure. Similar to Clear Quartz, the different colors of Jasper each have their own properties in addition to the above.

- **Malachite:** This beautiful deep emerald green crystal is a very powerful stone, but it needs to be handled with caution because it is toxic. It should only be used in its polished form, and if it is used to make an elixir, it should not be placed directly in the water. We will talk about making elixirs a little later.

  This magical stone amplifies positive and negative energies and grounds spiritual energies onto the planet. It clears and activates the chakras and attunes to spiritual guidance. Placed on the heart, it will bring balance and harmony and open the heart to unconditional love; placing it on the solar plexus brings deep emotional healing, releasing old traumas and negative experiences. If it is placed on the third eye, it will activate visualization and psychic vision, and it can be used for scrying.

  As a healing stone it is extremely versatile. It can be used to lower blood pressure, treat arthritis, swollen joints, fractures, tumors, epilepsy, vertigo, travel sickness, and much more. If worn around the waist it treats diabetes and it can be used for relieving cramps, including menstrual cramps. It has also been called the "midwife stone" because it resonates with the female productive organs and facilitates childbirth.

Because it is so powerful, it can sometimes cause heart palpitations if placed or worn on the body. If this happens, remove it immediately and neutralize its energy by replacing it with Rose Quartz or Rhodonite for a while.

- **Moonstone:** If you're drawn by the energy of the moon, you probably already have one of these. Moonstones are often milky white in color, but they can also be yellow, blue, or green. As the name suggests, this stone has a strong connection with the moon and intuition. It promotes empathy and encourages lucid dreaming, especially when the moon is full.

  Moonstone is a calming stone. It can be used to treat shock and calm hyperactive children. It soothes stress and emotional instability and improves emotional intelligence. Moonstone brings deep emotional healing and placing it on the solar plexus will help draw out old emotional patterning so that it can be understood and resolved. It also has a powerful effect on the female productive cycle and alleviates menstrual problems. It balances the hormonal systems, stabilizes fluid imbalances, and helps the digestive system. Wearing the stone to bed can prevent sleepwalking, and a moonstone elixir will help cure insomnia.

- **Obsidian:** This powerful stone works extremely fast because it has no boundaries or limitations. Obsidian is natural volcanic glass that is formed by molten lava that cooled so quickly that there was no time for it to crystallize. You will find it in a variety of colors, but watch out if you go crystal shopping; some of the blue-green colors can be manufactured glass.

Because of its shiny, reflective surface, it is also perfect for scrying.

This stone mercilessly exposes flaws, blockages, and weaknesses. Nothing is hidden from obsidian as it examines and exposes the causes behind emotional and physical problems. It could cause negative emotions and unpleasant truths to unexpectedly come rushing to the surface, and this could be overwhelming for some, so caution is advised. This stone brings strong protection by forming a shield against negativity. It has grounding properties and absorbs negative energies from the environment. On a spiritual level, it will vitalize the soul purpose and it anchors the soul in the body. Mentally, it brings clarity to the mind and expands the consciousness, and psychologically, it will bring you face-to-face with who you truly are.

As a healing tool, this stone can be used to promote physical digestion and to relieve joint pain, arthritis, and cramps. It detoxifies and dissolves blockages including hardened arteries. For those interested in the deities, this stone is also sacred to Hecate, the goddess of witches.

- **Tiger's eye:** This pretty stone is very popular and easy to get hold of and you will often find it in rings, brooches, and bracelets. The most common color for this stone is a beautiful brown and gold that reminds one of a tiger's eye, hence its name, but you will also find it in gold, pink, blue, and red.

The Tiger's Eye combines the energy of the sun with the earth's energy to create a high vibrational state that grounds and draws the spiritual energies to the earth. One of its main purposes is to protect, and traditionally it was carried as a talisman against curses and ill wishes. If placed on the third eye, it will balance the lower chakras and enhance psychic abilities.

When used for healing, this stone will heal the reproductive organs and throat, help with repairing broken bones, and dissolve constrictions.

- **Fluorite:** This stone is quite common and can be clear, blue, green, purple, brown, or yellow, or even a mixture of all of these. It is a highly protective stone, and will help you discern outside influences that are working against you. It shuts off undue mental influence and blocks psychic manipulation. Fluorite is used to cleanse and stabilize the aura and if you put it near your computer, it will protect you from electromagnetic stress. Fluorite is also a powerful learning aid. It increases concentration and organizes and processes the information in your brain by linking the new information to what is already known. Physically, fluorite assists with balance and coordination.

  As a healing stone, Fluorite is very powerful for dealing with infections and disorders. It repairs DNA damage and benefits teeth, bones, and body cells. It can be used to treat colds, flu, and sinusitis. Stroked across the body towards the heart, it will relieve the pain of stiff joints, arthritis, rheumatism, and spinal injuries. It heals the skin, removes blemishes and wrinkles, and provides relief for the discomfort caused by shingles and other nerve-related pain. As an elixir, it provides powerful protection against viruses.

- **Citrine:** These crystals in their natural form are comparatively rare, and can be found in tumbled form, as a geode, a cluster, or a point. When you go shopping for one, take care that you don't end up with heat-treated amethyst, which is often sold as Citrine. Citrine is transparent and can be anything from a very light yellow to a yellowish-brown, or even a smoky gray-brown. Its main feature is its powerful cleansing and regeneration properties. This beautiful stone carries the power of the sun, making it energizing, warming, and creative. It is one of the few stones that never need to be cleansed.

  The main reason why this stone is included is that it is one of the stones of abundance and often used in spells. It attracts all good things such as wealth, prosperity and success, and while it encourages you to share, it also helps you to hold on to what you already have. But this is not all this wonderful crystal is capable of—Citrine enhances positivity and boosts feelings of joy. It raises self-esteem, self-confidence, and individuality. It revitalizes the mind, enhances concentration and encourages self-expression and creativity. It makes you less sensitive to negativity and criticism, and is great for overcoming fears, phobias, and even depression.

As a healing stone, Citrine can be used to stimulate the spleen, pancreas, and digestive system. It is helpful with eye problems, detoxifies the blood, increases circulation, and balances the thyroid. Because it is also an eliminator, it will relieve constipation and remove cellulite. It can be used to make an elixir that will balance hormones and improve menstrual and menopausal issues.

Making Crystal Elixirs

As we've already seen, everything in the universe vibrates at different frequencies. It is no different when it comes to crystals, and in fact, it is the frequency at which the crystal vibrates that gives it its healing properties and other special attributes.

A crystal elixir is a vibrational medicine that is prepared by immersing a crystal into water, either directly or indirectly. The water picks up the vibration of the stone and takes on its properties. So, when you drink a crystal or gem elixir, you are taking on the vibration of the crystal or gem from which the crystal was made.

- **The direct method:** The first method of making an elixir is the direct method. This method is suitable for crystals that do not have any toxic properties and it is important to make sure that you have checked this before going ahead.

  To make your elixir, start by cleansing the crystal that you want to use. There are many methods to do this, and we will discuss them below when we talk about caring for your crystals. However, if the crystal that you want to use does not mind getting wet, you can simply hold it under running water while you envision white light flowing over it.

  Make sure that your chosen crystal is water tolerant otherwise you will spoil it. Some of the less dense crystals will dissolve or crack and even some of the harder ones cannot be left in water for an extended period of time. If you're not sure, rather use the indirect method which will be described below.

  Your crystal is now cleansed, and the next step is to simply place it in a clean glass vessel and pour spring water over it. Leave it open in the sun for the day if you want it to receive solar energy or under the moonlight for the night if you want lunar energy.

  When your elixir is ready, strain it through filter paper to remove any dust and leaves or little bits of grass that may have fallen in while it was outside. Pour your elixir in a bottle up to two-thirds full. Top it up with vodka or brandy to preserve it. This is your 'mother' elixir.

To use, simply fill a smaller bottle with water and add about a dozen drops of your mother elixir. Even though your smaller bottle only contains a small amount of the mother elixir, it still carries over the vibrational signature of the original elixir and has exactly the same properties.

- **The indirect method:** The indirect method is used for crystals that are toxic or not resistant to water. The difference between this method and the direct method is simply that the crystal is not immersed directly in the water.

  Use the same bowl that you would use for the direct method and fill it with spring water but do not immerse the crystal yet. Take the crystal and put it in a glass or a glass jar that is tall enough to stick out above the level of the water.

  From here on, you can just follow the steps for the direct method. Malachite, Fluorite, Angelite, Celestite, Azurite, and Halite (rock salt) are just a few of the stones that should never be immersed directly into the water. Malachite in particular, is toxic and the elixir could be poisonous.

Caring for your crystals

Many crystals are fragile and can crumble easily while crystals that are clustered or layered can separate. Crystals that have been tumbled to a smooth finish have a tougher surface and can be kept together in a bag. Crystals that have been polished and not tumbled, or are still in their raw form can easily get damaged or scratched because of rough surfaces or sharp points and should be wrapped separately in silk or velvet cloth.

When you have just bought a new crystal or you've used one of your crystals, you should cleanse it before putting it away. If you receive a crystal or a piece of jewelry with a crystal in it as a gift, always cleanse it before wearing or using it to remove any energies that might be passed on to you.

There are few crystals that are self-cleansing and never need to be cleansed. These are as follows: Citrine, Kyanite, and Azeztulite. Clear Quartz and Carnelian can be used to cleanse other crystals, and this is especially handy for those delicate, friable crystals. A small crystal can be cleansed by putting it on a clear quartz crystal overnight, and if you pop a carnelian nugget into your bag with all your other tumbled crystals and you will never need to cleanse those crystals by any other method.

Cleansing is simple. If the crystal can handle water, hold it under a running tap while you visualize white light pouring over it. Hold the intention that all the negativity will be washed away and the stone reenergized. While some people immerse their stones in the ocean or in salty water, this is not recommended unless you are very sure that your crystal is resistant to the damaging effects that salt can have on it.

Another way to cleanse crystals is by putting them in the sunlight for a couple of hours. Remember that the sun does not stand still. It crosses the heavens in an arc, and you need to be careful that you position your crystal in such a way that it can't magnify the rays of the sun and cause a fire. Some crystals fade when in sunlight and these are better charged by the light of the moon.

Crystals that are in clusters or friable can be left overnight in sea salt or rock salt. If you do this, be sure to gently brush all traces of salt off the crystal after cleansing as it can cause damage if it is exposed to moisture.

Smudging is another method that you can use. Smudging is a method of purification originally used by Native Americans. It's simply the process of wafting about the smoke of slow-burning dried herbs. You can also pass the crystal through the light of a candle, or, if you're good with visualizing, you can visualize your crystals surrounded by light—this will also purify and energize them.

Essential Oils

Essential oils give plants their characteristic odor and are extracted from grasses, twigs, needles, seeds, peels of fruit, bark, and roots. These oils are popularly used for aromatherapy but they are also used in diffusers and humidifiers. Most oils can also be combined with a carrier oil such as coconut or avocado oil and applied to the skin.

How Essential Oils Are Produced

Essential oils are volatile, meaning that they evaporate easily at normal temperatures, so distillation is a very effective method of extracting these oils from most plant matter. Hydrodistillation is a method that has been in use for over a thousand years and is the simplest one. The plant matter is boiled in water and the water vapor is condensed back into liquid form through cooling. Essential oils float on water, so the water and oil can easily be separated.

Another form of distillation is steam distillation. The plant matter is placed in a closed chamber and steam is passed through it. This causes the volatile compounds in the plant to evaporate and release the oils. As with hydrodistillation, the oil and water are simply separated to complete the process.

There are some oils that are so sensitive to heat that they cannot be distilled; particularly the oils in the rinds of citrus fruits. These oils are mechanically extracted using a method called mechanical expression. The whole fruits are tossed around in a large mechanical container covered with lots of tiny spikes on the inside. These little spikes scratch and scar the skin to pierce the essential oil glands on the skin of the fruit and this releases the essential oils. The essential oil is then flushed away from the fruit with water, and in the final step, a centrifugal separator separates the oil from the water and any juice or fruit particles.

Some plant materials such as rose petals and jasmine flowers are too delicate to survive either of the above processes. Their oils are extracted using chemical solvents such as hexane and ethanol. Because of this, these oils are not considered to be truly essential oils. They contain heavier non-volatile molecules and are also more viscous than essential oils.

Ways to Use Essential Oils

One could easily assume that essential oils are gentle and harmless because they are so completely natural, but this is not quite true. Essential oils are highly concentrated and can be up to seventy-five times more powerful than dried herbs, so it is important to be aware of the properties of the essential oil you are using.

Essential oils can be used to relieve headaches, soothe muscle inflammation, promote healthy sleep, treat colds, improve skin conditions, and aid with indigestion. You can use them in personal care and cleaning products, and you can use them simply to make your home or office smell good.

- **Inhalation:** The easiest way to use an essential oil is to inhale it by removing the top of the bottle and breathing in. Don't let the undiluted oil touch your skin because it could cause irritation or even burn you.

- **Dry evaporation:** Put a drop on a piece of cotton wool or absorbent material and leave it in your car, hang it in a cupboard, or keep it in your pocket and take a sniff when you feel like it.

- **Using a humidifier:** The most important thing when using a humidifier is making sure that it is suitable for the use of essential oils. Simply add a drop to the water tank and the aroma will naturally be released into the room along with the vapor. Clean your humidifier regularly to make sure that there is no oil residue that can clog and damage it.

- **Diluted:** Add a couple of drops of essential oil to your body wash or shampoo and conditioner. If you like to shower, dab a drop or two on the walls of the shower or use diluted on a washcloth. For a relaxing, aromatic bath, combine a few drops of your favorite essential oil with coconut oil and add it to your bathwater—don't put it in the bath without mixing it with a carrier oil as it is likely to stain your bath.

- **Using essential oil on your skin:** Essential oil should never be applied to the skin without first being diluted with a carrier oil. Create your own recipe with your favorite oils and use it to massage away muscle pain, tension, and stiffness. For stress relief, and even if you're just tired, rub some of your mixture on your temples, wrists, and third eye. Take special care when putting essential oils on your face. Make sure that they are sufficiently diluted with a carrier oil so that they do not burn or irritate your skin.

There is a wide array of essential oils to choose from, and each has its own special properties. To get you started, let's take a look at some of the most popular ones:

Tea tree oil: While this is not the most aromatic of essential oils, its benefits make it a must-have for your collection. Tea tree oil can be used to treat warts, acne, nail fungus, cuts, septic wounds, ringworm, carbuncles, ringworm, and other skin conditions.

Peppermint oil: Muscle pain, headaches, colds, nausea, sinus, and a variety of other conditions can be treated with peppermint oil. Because of its potent, yet pleasant flavor, it is popular for use in mouthwashes, breath fresheners, soaps, shampoos, and a variety of other products.

Lemon oil: Because of its refreshing aroma, lemon oil is popular for use in humidifiers but it also boosts immunity, improves circulation, combats fatigue, and helps fight depression. It can also be very useful for treating skin conditions, but should not be used on parts of the skin that are exposed to sunlight as it can cause burns.

Lavender oil: Lavender is one of the most popular essential oils because of its calming floral aroma and because it is so versatile. Because of its soothing and relaxing effect it is one of the best remedies for insomnia. It has antiseptic, antifungal and anti-inflammatory properties and can be used as an antidepressant or for migraine headaches, toothache, nerve pain, and sprains. Lavender oil can be found in bath products, body oils and lotions, hair products, air fresheners, and a wide variety of other products.

Eucalyptus oil: The vibrant, minty, pine scent of eucalyptus is great for clearing your chest if you inhale its vapor and it will also relieve coughing if rubbed on the chest and throat. But that is not the only purpose for this oil. If you mix it with a little bit of lemon and add it to your diffuser, it will keep those pesky mosquitoes at bay. Make a salve with eucalyptus oil and put it on cold sores to reduce pain and inflammation and speed up the healing process. Combined with a carrier oil, eucalyptus can be used as a massage oil to relieve muscle pain and treat conditions like rheumatoid arthritis and osteoarthritis.

Rosemary oil: Its refreshing properties are what makes this oil so popular, and it has a multitude of uses. Added to your shampoo, it can relieve an itchy scalp and prevent hair loss. A dab on the brow will relieve a mild headache, and a drop in your diffuser will keep mosquitoes at bay. Rosemary oil is also known for relieving stress but its most interesting property is its ability to improve concentration and memory if it is inhaled. Researchers have done studies where it was proven that students who were in a room diffused with rosemary oil fared up to seven percent better in memory tests than students who had not been exposed to the aroma.

Frankincense: The lesser-known name for frankincense is Olibanum. This essential oil is made from the resin of the Boswellia tree that typically can be found in Africa, India, and the Middle East. The name of the oil is derived from the French expression, "franc encens," which means "high-quality incense." In Old French the word "franc" meant "pure" or "noble."

The earthy, spicy, woody smell of frankincense has a calming effect making it popular for use during meditation or yoga. As an astringent, it reduces the appearance of wrinkles and discoloration of the skin. It stimulates the growth of new skin cells so is great for cuts and abrasions. As an inhalant, it provides relief for congestion and encourages easy breathing.

A few things to keep in mind when using essential oils

Essential oils are potent and, if used incorrectly, they could be harmful so they should always be used responsibly and with care.

- Essential oils should never be ingested.
- Because of their potency, essential oils could be harmful to young children, the elderly, pregnant women, and women who are breastfeeding, so oils should be sufficiently diluted if they are used, and wintergreen and birch oil should be avoided completely.

- Some essential oils can be harmful to animals, so if you have pets, first make sure that the oil you are using is safe for your furry, fluffy, and feathered companions as well.

- If you have health concerns or are taking medications for conditions such as epilepsy or high blood pressure you should check with your health practitioner first before using essential oils.

The Witch's Knife

Traditionally, the one tool that every witch owned was a boline, and even today, many witches will cringe at the idea of grabbing any old kitchen knife to cut herbs, inscribe candles, cut cords, draw spell circles, and do other witchy things. A boline is a knife with a small, straight or crescent-shaped blade. Traditionally, it has a white handle but there are no rules about that for the witch of today. It is your personal choice and you could even find a wonderfully ornate knife that suits your purpose perfectly. It is a popular belief that this tool should be used as often as possible because that way it accumulates magical power.

Another kind of knife that witches have, but seldom use for purposes other than spell casting and ceremonies, is the athame. Traditionally this is a dagger with a predominantly black handle, but again, it doesn't matter what color it is or what it looks like as long as you like it.

Some traditional witches make their own knives, and while the process is not too complicated, it is not always easy to get hold of the materials and tools to do it in today's times. Many witches also do not have the

space for that kind of work. If you do want to make your own knife, simply search online for instructions and go ahead.

All tools, whether they have been bought, gifted to you, or made, should be cleansed and purified to remove any negative vibrations before you use it. This can be done in any way that you feel comfortable with. You can rinse it under running water and visualize white light pouring over it the same way you cleanse your crystals. Another way is to wipe it with a special cloth towards the tip. Imagine that the cloth has collected all the negative energy and then shake it out and picture the negative energy turning into something beautiful like flowers or butterflies. It doesn't really matter how you do it, or what you do, as long as you are comfortable with yourself. Modern magick only has one rule, and that is to always keep the greater good in mind and do no harm.

Wands

Wands are naturally associated with witches and are one of the prime tools of witchcraft. The popular Harry Potter series of fantasy witchcraft novels by British author J.K. Rowling spurned a huge interest in this little stick—it also created loads of misperceptions and some witchcraft shops have even been slammed for refusing to sell their wands to Harry Potter fans. Many witches have wands, but you will seldom see them, or, if they are on display, the message will come across very clearly: "Don't touch!" Wands are very personal to the witches who own them and can be considered one of the "sacred tools" of both modern and ancient witchcraft.

Many witches today own more than one wand and you can also make a wand to serve a single purpose and then destroy it. It's your magick and your wand, so you can do with it as you please. Contrary to what many people think, wands are not just used for invocations and casting spells. They also have a wide variety of purposes when it comes to healing, chakra cleansing and other energy practices.

Traditionally wands were made from the wood of a sacred tree such as apple, birch, willow, peach, hazel, or cherry, and its length had to be from the crook of the elbow to the middle of the index finger. However, apart from the three immutable universal laws, there are no hard and fast rules for today's witch. If you go to a witchcraft shop you will find wands made of metal, wood, crystal, and many other modern materials, but you don't have to buy a wand. You can make your own using any material that you please. Your wand could be a stick that 'called' to you when you went on a walk one day and you just had to pick it up, or you could make something really fancy. You could wrap it in leather or other natural material, carve runes or spells into it and tip or decorate it with crystals. Think of the purpose you want to use it for and let your intuition guide you when you make it, and it will always be perfect.

Other Tools

Along with herbs, crystals, essential oils, wands, and knives, there are a myriad of other tools that witches can use to practice their craft. Tools for divination include crystal balls, tarot and oracle cards of almost every kind, yarrow sticks, runes, pendulums, and more. For casting spells, you can use candles, little pieces of string, paper, leaves, shells, hair, stones, bones, and literally anything else you can get your hands on.

Some witches like to have specialized tools that are specifically dedicated to their craft. You might want to buy a cauldron or a chalice or a pentagram, or wear a specific robe and stand a broom made of sticks in the corner when you're practicing your craft. That's entirely up to you.

To practice your craft and to be a witch, you don't need fancy tools. In fact, you don't need any tools at all. The most important part of being a witch and practicing magick is not the tools that you use. It is in discovering that you are the instrument and source of your own personal brand of magick.

Chapter 3: Spells

Stage magicians, movies, folklore, and fairytales have created a perception that spells are cast by pointing or waving a wand at the object or person the spell is intended to affect while shouting "Hocus Pocus, Alakazam!" or "Abra Cadabra!" at the top of your voice. There should be at least a puff of smoke, but preferably a light rumble of thunder and a bolt of lightning as evidence that the spell is effectively cast.

We all know this is not true, but many of us have no idea how you really cast a spell and how to make it work. We will be looking at this as well as the tools that you can use as aids for casting your spells. And of course, we will look at some simple spells that you can try out.

Before "casting off"

There are a few things that you need to know so that you can practice this part of your craft responsibly and so that your spells will work.

Before using magick to help yourself or another person, you need to first make sure that there is nothing practical that can be done to solve the problem. If a person comes to you asking for a spell to help them find a life partner, first make sure that this is really what they need. Maybe they lack the self-confidence to go out and meet people, or they're just shy. Then a spell to boost their self-confidence would be a much better option. The modern witch often ends up being a coach or counselor as well as a witch.

It is also very important to make sure that the changes you wish to make are truly for the good of all those who will be affected by them. Sally may want you to help her get the attention of a young man, but the young man has a girlfriend. Obviously getting the young man's attention might be good for Sally, but the girlfriend will suffer. This is a very simple example, but it clearly illustrates that you need to look carefully at all the angles before casting a spell.

The essence of magick

It has been said several times now that you don't really need tools to do magick. The magick is right there inside of you. But if you don't know how to make work, it is useless.

Remember that a witch is someone who is aligned with the energies of the universe. Be reminded also, that there are seven laws of the universe.

These laws affect the universe and everything that is in it, including you. And finally, remember that the law of attraction encompasses these seven laws and that an understanding of this law will open the door to understanding all the other laws.

The law of attraction is easy to understand once you 'get' the basic concept. Sometimes we struggle to understand something because we expect it to be way more complicated than it is. We refuse to accept that something so incredible can be so simple and straightforward and keep searching for some kind of "deeper meaning." That is often the case with the law of attraction. There is no "deeper meaning." In a nutshell, the law of attraction means that you get what you're thinking about, whether you wanted it or not. That's it.

Everything in the universe vibrates at its own frequency. Positive emotions such as joy, and positive thoughts, actions, words, and intentions vibrate at a much higher frequency than negative emotions such as anger, hatred, spite, and so on, which all have lower, much baser vibrations. The more you focus on positive words, thoughts, and deeds, the higher it raises your vibration in the universe and the more likely it becomes that you will attract positive things into your life.

People who achieve their goals are constantly thinking about them, talking about them, and working towards them. These thoughts, deeds, and actions create vibrations that become stronger and stronger every time the person thinks about or does something towards achieving their goal. Their personal vibration becomes infused with the vibration of what they are constantly focused on, and the universal vibration answers this call by sending things that vibrate at the same frequency.

When you set your intention to get what you want, this knowledge; along with knowing how to choose the right words, is what will make your spells work. When stating your wants or needs to the universe, you have to speak the "language of the universe" or you will be misunderstood and get what you didn't want rather than what you wanted. You may think you are focusing on what you want, but if you are using the wrong words, you are standing in your own way, and your spells won't work.

Here's a simple example: You're casting a spell to help you lose weight. You've designed your own spell and you chant: "Hear, hear, let my fat disappear!" It is not because it's a 'silly' spell that you're not going to get what you want. It's because the words of your spell include the thing that you want to disappear. You are thinking about fat, so the universe will give you more of that. To get what you want, you have to focus on what you *want;* not on what you *don't* want. If your spell had said: "Ahoy, ahoy, I'm healthy, slim, and full of joy," your chances of losing weight immediately increase by a hundred percent.

There are as many kinds of spells as you can think of things to cast spells for. You can cast banishing and binding spells, spells for fertility, a spell to help someone get a promotion at work, protection spells, good fortune spells, spells for the seasons, and more. While it is quite alright to replace an item in a spell with something else, do remember that each item used in a spell has certain significance because of its vibration or special properties. As you know by now, there are no hard and fast rules for anything magick, and you can easily create your own spells by following a few simple guidelines. In fact, if you do, your spell will be even more powerful because you were focused on what you wanted while you were creating it.

Let's do some 'spelling!'

Prepare your sacred space

Before casting any spell you need to prepare a sacred space where you can perform your magick. A space created for spiritual activity is called a sacred space, and because magick draws on spiritual knowledge in order to effect change, it is considered a spiritual activity. You don't need a separate room for this. All you need to do is to claim a specific place somewhere in your home where you will not be disturbed for the duration of the spell. When you're done, you can return the space to its original state. If possible, clear your space in the center of the room because energy can get trapped in corners and disturb the vibration you want to create.

You need an area large enough so that you can sit in the center of it with some space to move. It is up to you to decide whether you want to cleanse the area with salt and water beforehand and whether you wish to place candles around you or not. While it is true that the vibrations of these items can help raise the vibration of your magick, they are not essential. The only thing you really need is your *intention*.

Now that your space is ready, you need to cast a "circle of light." This is to ground and protect you, and so that you can invoke the four elements that sustain life: Earth, Air, Water, and Fire. You can use a crystal, a wand, or your forefinger. Point your chosen item outwards and 'draw' the circle clockwise, starting and ending in the direction that the sun sets in your part of the world— east if you're in the northern hemisphere and west if you're on the upside-down side of the planet! Draw the energy of the earth up through your feet, through your body, up your arm, and let it escape through your finger or wand. As you do this, imagine that you are filling the room with white light.

The vibration of the spoken word carries a lot of power, so when the circle is complete, you should declare it cast. There is no need for fancy words and 'high' English with all the 'thees' and 'thous' that go with it. It is about your intention. When you say it, put your heart in it and believe that what you are saying is so and that it manifests as you speak. Use simple words in plain English or use the language that you are comfortable in. State the purpose of the circle and declare that it is so by adding the phrase, "as above, so below" to affirm the Law of Correspondence which states that the physical, spiritual, and mental realms are in correspondence, harmony and agreement with each other.

Here's a suggestion: "I hereby declare that this circle that I have conjured will protect me from all harm while I am busy with my spiritual practice. As above, so below." that's it. Your circle is cast and you can now proceed with casting your spell.

The spells shared with you are simple spells for the beginner with little or no experience in the craft of magick. They are not 'recipes' with specific ingredients and instructions, but rather ideas of how to create your own spells with what you have on hand. Always remember when creating your spells that it is about the *intention*, not the tool. If you do your 'spelling' with respect and love, the universe will reward you in like currency.

- **Guardian Spell to Protect Your Home**

  When you think about your home, one of the most important things is that it should be a place where you can feel safe and protected. The practice of setting up magical safeguards around your home or at your front door is one of the oldest traditions of magick.

  You can use anything from a plant to a crystal to a figurine of a deity or totem animal. If you wish, you can also make your own figurine out of clay or wax or whatever you choose. The figurine or plant symbolizes your protector. Because this is a protection spell, your protector will need a weapon—something that symbolizes protection. Typically, thorns or nails are used, but you can use anything you like. If your figurine carries its own sword, that's also good.

  If you choose a plant it should be the thorniest cactus you can find. Use what attracts you, and remember, it's about the *intention*, not the tool.

  Now that you have your protector and it is properly armed, the next step is to dedicate it to its purpose. Put it in front of you in your circle and center yourself. Focus all your intention on the object and visualize as clearly as possible how you are protected against all harm. You might want to picture your home covered by a dome guarded by the object, or you may imagine your figurine storming gallantly into battle to defend your honor and safety. Do whatever works for you. While you are visualizing, you can say something that states the intention that you wish to manifest. You could make a rhyme, or just use plain words in your chosen language. Here's an idea:

"Defend and protect this home,
and all that within it may roam.
I dedicate you to this task.
Do it well, is all I ask."

To seal your spell, affirm the Law of Correspondence by saying, "as above, so below; as below, so above." Now, take your dedicated item and bury it near your front gate or at your front door, or walk around your garden until you find the 'right' spot. If it is a plant, do the same, but make sure that the place you put it is a safe spot where it can't accidentally 'protect' you from an innocent person!

• Severing Spell to Break Ties With the Past

Sometimes it's hard to move on after a broken relationship or maybe losing a friend. We cannot move forward if we cannot let go of the past, but this is not always easy. This spell can help break those ties with the past that hold us back, but it will not work if the person doesn't have a true desire to let go and move on. No spell can change your will.

To do this spell you will need to tie a knot at either end of a length of cord, string, ribbon, or whatever calls to you. The knots represent the future and the past, respectively. You will also need a candle and a fireproof dish. These will be used to sever the cord and burn one half of it. Myrrh is sometimes used to symbolize death while saffron is used to represent love, healing, happiness and strength, so, if you can get hold of these two in incense form, you can add them to your tool-kit for this spell.

The best time to cast this spell is on the dark moon as this is a powerful time for endings and new beginnings. Always start with casting your sacred circle first. When you are ready, light the candle and state your intention. You can say something like:

"By this token
I am set free
from the past
that was holding me.
Into the future
I now go.
As above,
so below;
as below,
so above"

Light the myrrh to represent the final death of the relationship or issue. Take the cord and hold one of the knots in each hand; the left hand represents the past, and the right, the future. Now hold the knot over the candle and state your intention again while you allow it to burn all the way through. Once the cord is completely severed, put the 'future' knot aside and continue to burn the rest of the 'past' cord to ashes in the fireproof dish. Extinguish the myrrh and light the saffron. Now take the remaining piece of cord that represents the future and hold it over the saffron until it is permeated with the smell. Take the ashes of the 'past' cord and blow them into the wind in the direction of the sunset. Keep the 'future' cord on you, bury it in the garden, or put it on your special altar. It's up to you.

• A Spell to Aid Communication

Communication in any relationship is very important but sometimes people find it hard to put their feelings into words, or they are just hesitant to discuss matters that are troubling them. A reluctance to communicate can lead to misunderstandings because it leaves the other person to assume or guess what the problem is. This spell is to encourage partners, friends, and even colleagues to be more open and communicative with each other.

You are going to make a paper chain so you will need nine strips of paper, each about five inches long and one inch wide, and glue or Scotch tape to make your loops. You will also need green ink and a feather that you have made into a writing quill—instructions on how to do this can be found online. If you can't find green ink or do not feel like making a quill, you can use any tool that can write in green such as a green crayon or felt tip pen, but you will still need the feather. Finally, you will need a candle and lavender incense.

We call on the element of Air for this spell as this element provides energy towards communication and connection. The feather symbolizes Air, and if you do take the trouble to make a quill it will increase the power of your spell. The reason we are using green ink is that the color green supports magical workings related to relationships and changing attitudes along with some other things. The best time to cast this spell is on a Wednesday when the moon is waxing as this eases communication. Wednesday is also sacred to Mercury, the messenger of the gods.

As always, begin by preparing your sacred circle. When you are ready, light the candle and use it to light the lavender incense—lavender protects relationships.

Use your chosen writing tool to write your name in green on one of the strips of paper. On the other one, write the name or names of the people with whom you want to open the communication channels. On each of the remaining seven strips, write one of the following words: *Trust, Listen, Speak, Look, Touch, Give, Receive.*

Make the first loop of your paper chain using the strip with your name on it. The next seven links are the strips with the words on them, and your final link is the paper with your partner, friend, or colleague's name. All the writing should show inward. Hold your completed chain in your hands and use the feather to waft the lavender incense over it while you seal your spell with words. For this spell you might want to say something to the tune of:

"Element of air, let it be. Open the channels of communication between [name] and me."

And then, as always, end with "as above, so below; as below, so above" Hang your chain in the area where you spend the most time with this person, preferably in front of a window so that the light shines through it.

• A Spell for Material Prosperity

Before casting this spell, make sure that you understand what it is for or you may be disappointed. The universe does not see material prosperity the way most people see it. To the universe, material prosperity means that you are comfortable and have enough of everything that you need. The universe does not understand 'want' and will not cater to greed, so it will not work to get you that brand new model car or designer jacket. However, it will ensure that you always have clothing on your back, a roof over your head, and food in your tummy. If you don't have a car and you really need one, or if your car is really old and needs to be replaced, it will help you with that. The universe is an infinite store of everything that you ever may require, and that is why it will never give you more than what you need.

Now that you understand what this spell is for, let's go ahead and 'spell!' You will need six mint leaves—pineapple mint is best, but any mint is good enough, a length of golden-colored cord or ribbon, six drops of mint essential oil combined with a tablespoon of almond carrier oil, and a green candle. Mint is always useful in prosperity spells, but pineapple mint with its almost golden appearance, is known for bringing prosperity from unexpected sources, which is why it is preferred. The cord or ribbon is a golden color because gold is full of magickal energy and enhances the ability to send energy where it is directed. The candle is green because prosperity, fertility, money, and luck are all represented by this color. You may have noticed that we have six mint leaves and six drops of mint oil. The number six is related to the energy of the sun. It has a strong masculine vibration and is connected to security and responsibility.

The best time to do this spell is when the moon is waxing—you will notice that spells where you wish to draw something towards you are mostly done during this phase of the moon. It is best not to do this spell on a Saturday because restrictive Saturn rules this day.

Start by casting your sacred circle. Once you're settled and centered, anoint your candle with the peppermint and almond oil. This is how you do it: Hold the candle loosely in your left hand. Dip the index and middle fingers of your right hand in the oil mixture and stroke oil onto the candle with an upwards motion. Stop just before you get to the top, and reverse the direction going all the way back to the base. Turn the candle a little bit and repeat the process six times so that the candle is covered in oil. End the anointing by stopping halfway down instead of going all the way down on the last stroke. While you're doing the anointing, visualize the outcome of the spell—see yourself in the position that you wish to be, not the position that you are. That is very important, because the universe looks at the 'picture' in your mind and gives you what it sees, remember?

Light your candle and say:

"Infinite source of abundance,
I open myself to thee.
So that all that I require,
may manifest for me."

Use the golden cord or ribbon to tie your mint leaves together by their stems in a tight bundle and wave them over the candle while you seal your spell with these words:

"Let me prosper;
let me grow.
As above,
so below;
as below,
so above"

Keep your leaves in your wallet or purse. Growing mint around your home will help to maintain the power of this spell.

• A Knotty Spell for Knotty Problems

Sometimes there is a problem that is so complex that you don't have the foggiest notion of where or how to even begin to unravel it, much less solve it. It could be a relationship problem, an issue at work, or even something practical such as designing a complicated mechanism. Problems like these are often called 'knotty' problems or issues, and what better spell then, than a spell with knots in it?

You will need rosemary incense; a length of string as long as your forearm from the crook of your elbow to your wrist, and a light blue candle. The rosemary incense brings clarity and the blue candle signifies wisdom, guidance, and perception. You can cast this spell any time between the full moon and the new moon.

As always, start by casting your sacred circle. Light the candle and use its flame to light the incense. While you're doing this, say:

"Flickering flame
and light of day,
light my path;
and show me the way."

Take an end of the string in each hand and move it over the incense so that the whole string has been exposed to the smoke. You will now tie seven knots in the string; one for each day of the week. As you tie your knots, say the lines below for each corresponding knot:

"One for the sun to illuminate
Two for the moon to investigate
Three for an eye to help me see
Four to find the power in me
Five to end all my confusion
Six to show me the obvious solution
Seven to bring it all to conclusion."

For the next seven nights, put the string under your pillow. Before you go to sleep; starting with the first knot you made, untie one knot each night while thinking about the reason you're doing this in the first place. As each day goes by, the problem will begin to unravel itself and you will begin to find clarity as you near the end of the ritual.

Remember, you have asked a question, so you must keep your eyes and ears open for the answer. Because this is a sleep-ritual, the answer is likely to come to you in your dreams, so take note of them—literally. Keep a notepad beside your bed so that you can make notes of your dreams as soon as you wake up, no matter what time it is. Sometimes we wake up from a dream in the middle of the night. At that moment, we're sure we'll remember it, so we turn over and go back to sleep, but when we wake up the next morning; poof, it's gone. However, this is not the only way your answer will come, so be aware and look out for signals from the universe.

Crafting your own spells

There are hundreds of books with spells for almost anything you can think of, and you will seldom find two books with exactly the same spells. This is because a spell is not like a recipe to bake a cake. For a cake, you need to make sure that you have the right ingredients in exactly the right quantities. You have to follow a certain procedure when you mix it, and you have to bake it at a certain temperature or your cake will be a flop. A spell is something different. A spell is created by a witch to serve a purpose, so that particular witch will choose the elements that they feel will work best to serve that purpose, often using what they have on hand. These spells are then written down and passed on for other witches to use. Each element in a spell has its own specific vibration, so the elements will be chosen with the purpose of creating the highest vibration possible towards the purpose of the spell.

A spell is like a prayer or an affirmation—it is the act of creating a vibration in the universe to attract something that you want. It is something personal to you, and the more personal you make it, the more effective it is.

The thought that you have a need for something starts the vibration. This vibration becomes stronger if you verbally express that need because your voice is created by the vibration of the vocal cords. Each word you speak vibrates at its own frequency, so if you use positive words with high vibrations, it increases the vibration even more. When you take a physical action towards fulfilling your need, the vibration becomes even stronger, and when you cast a spell and focus your intent on the outcome, you enhance that vibration even more.

To help you understand this even better, let's do a little experiment. Take a large, round plastic dish and place it on the floor. Fill it with water almost up to the rim. You will need a handful of pebbles or marbles that will sink when you drop them into the water.

Wait until the water is completely still before you begin your experiment. When the water is completely still, take a pebble and drop it into the center of the dish from a height of about twelve inches above the surface of the water. Watch how it causes ripples that spread across the surface. As soon as the first ripple hits the edge of the dish, drop in the next one. Try to drop the pebbles in more or less for the same spot every time. As you keep dropping the pebbles, you will see that the ripples will become waves. Keep going until the waves are so big that they cause the water to splash over the rim of the dish.

The water represents the universe. The pebbles each represent a thought, deed, word, intention, action, and anything else you do that is directed towards your goal. Your goal is represented by the center of the dish and the waves represent the vibrations you are creating with the pebbles you're dropping. That is why you had to keep aiming for the same spot. The more accurate you are, and the more frequently you drop your pebbles, the quicker the waves will begin to splash over the rim, illustrating how your actions, words, and thoughts contribute to strengthening the 'want' vibration.

There are no specific rules to follow when you craft your own spells, but just like buildings, regardless of their design, have to adhere to the basic principles of engineering in order to be sturdy and remain standing, spells also have a common foundation that contribute to their success:

Determine the purpose of your spell:

- *Who will benefit from the spell?* Do not cast spells that affect people who have not given you permission to cast a spell on them. The spell should be for you or someone who has asked you to cast a spell on their behalf.

- *What do you want the spell to do?* What do you want from it? Be as specific as possible. For instance, let's assume that there's always too much month left at the end of your money. You do all that you can to make ends meet, but it's always a struggle. Asking for a "better life" doesn't really say much. You need to be way more specific than that. Think of ways that your problem can be solved. Do you need an increase, or maybe a job with a better salary? Or do you just need to learn how to manage what you have?

- *State your purpose.* Always strive for something positive and never use negative words such as 'won't,' 'can't,' or 'don't.' Focus on what you do want, not on what you don't want. Remember the example of losing weight?

- *Break it down.* If your goal is complex, break it down into smaller steps and address each step with a specific spell.

- *Get your timing right.* Choose the best timing for your spell. As you may have noted above, some spells are better cast when the moon is waxing while the power of other spells is increased by the full moon. The day of the week or month is also significant, so make sure that you choose a day and date that vibrates in tune with your desire.

Craft your spell:

A spell is usually composed of:

1. An item that creates energy and light such as a candle—the color of your candle can strengthen your spell, and you can also carve symbols onto it and anoint it with essential oil.

2. A sensory element such as incense or essential oil—look for an aroma that resonates with your requirement.

3. Objects that symbolize our desire—this could be anything from a wallet stuffed with fake banknotes to seashells,

feathers, rose petals, crystals, or even a toy. A tiny teddy bear could symbolize security, and a toy car could represent the car that you need or a trip. Search for objects that resonate with your need or desire; follow your instinct when it comes to this and you're bound to come up with exactly what you need. In the prosperity spell above we used mint leaves for their gold color. If an object is associated with something over a long period of time, that object will take on the vibration of the association. Because gold and mint have been associated with prosperity throughout the ages, their vibrations resonate with the idea of prosperity.

4. Words to state your intention—this is the incantation or spell. Some words have more power than others because of their vibration, but, contrary to popular belief, there are no 'magic' words.

   Your spell needn't be fancy and it doesn't have to rhyme. Nor does it have to contain a whole lot of "thees" and "thous" or "so mote it be's." Just choose your words in plain English or the language that you are most comfortable in; make sure that they are positive, and that they clearly state your need or desire. Seal your spell by saying "as above, so below" or "amen" or "so be it," or you can make a gesture. As long as it means "it will be" it doesn't matter what words you use. The universe doesn't speak a human language—it simply picks up the vibration of the image or emotion in your mind and responds to that.

5. Physical actions—wafting incense smoke over something, tying a knot, burying an object, and so on. Just like thoughts and words, physical actions strengthen the vibration of our spell. Whatever action you choose, keep your intention focused when you perform it. If you are burying something in the garden for your spell, there's no point in doing it while you're thinking of what to make for dinner.

Remember that casting your spell is the act of creating a vibration in the universe to draw towards you that which you desire. It is a part of the process, not the whole process. You have to reinforce that vibration constantly with your actions. If you've cast a spell to find a partner, sitting at home waiting for the phone to ring, or for someone on social media to notice you is not the kind of action that will support a positive outcome. However, if you were to go out, join a dating club, spend time with friends, and make an effort to get out there and meet people, you are helping to create circumstances that are conducive to a positive outcome and you will get what you desire.

Chapter 4: Discover Your Psychic Abilities

If you've ever had a feeling in your gut that something is going to happen, and it does, you've experienced your sixth sense—your psychic power, or as some call it, intuition. Realizing that you have knowledge about something without knowing how you gained that knowledge is another sign that indicates that your psychic powers are active. You could be talking with someone, and suddenly you realize that they are deceiving you, or you pick up an emotion such as sadness from them. That's another sure sign that your psychic abilities are "switched on."

We confidently use our five senses—sight, taste, smell, hearing, and touch, but when it comes to the sixth sense, we're a little less sure of ourselves. It's in human nature to be wary of things that we don't fully understand, and people with psychic abilities were often feared and even persecuted. Even in today's times, some people eye these abilities with suspicion and condemn psychic activities.

Everybody is born with all six senses, but in some people not all the senses are activated. Some people are born blind or without the ability to hear or speak; one could consider these abilities "switched off" in these people. The same goes for the sixth sense. Not everybody is born with their psychic ability "switched on," but almost everybody has the ability to develop it to at least some extent if they are interested and willing to make some effort. It's a bit like learning to play a musical instrument. Even if you aren't an extremely talented musician; if you are interested enough to learn and make an effort to practice and keep on working at it, you could become good enough to at least perform at the local talent show.

The Four Kinds of Psychic Ability

- *Clairvoyance* is 'seeing' on a psychic level. It describes the ability to see forms that vibrate at a frequency that makes them invisible to someone who doesn't have this ability to 'see.' These forms are popularly referred to as spirits, but that isn't necessarily what they are. It is also the ability to receive mental messages consciously or subconsciously transmitted by others.

- *Clairaudience* is 'hearing' on a psychic level. This ability is similar to clairvoyance, only it involves hearing voices and sounds rather than seeing forms. Telepathy falls under this category. Clairaudience and clairvoyance often work together, so the person will both 'hear' and 'see.'

- *Clairsentience* is the ability to tune into the vibration of a person and 'feel' what they are feeling. Intuitive feelings such as hunches and the ability to immediately pick up the atmosphere when entering a room fall in this category.

- *Claircognizance* is the ability to receive information or impressions by way of an instinctive knowing, without having to be told, or read about it. It is almost as if it is 'remembered' from an outside source.

Developing your psychic skills takes time and practice, and it's not possible to cover everything you need to know in an introductory book such as this one. We will be looking at a few psychic practices such as scrying, dowsing, and card reading to introduce you to this fascinating "other dimension" and give you a chance to see how "switched on" your psychic talents are.

This book discourages occult practices such as trying to communicate with spirits or other entities. Séances are not tea parties and Ouija boards and other summoning tools are not toys that can be experimented with. Summoning spirits is dangerous, even for those with a lot of experience in such matters. It is also completely unnecessary to disturb spirits who were not disturbing you. The universe is an infinite source of knowledge, and your mind is part of the Universal Mind, so the answer to every question you will ever ask is already available to you. You must just know how to find it.

I Scry With My Inner Eye...

It's part of human nature to want to have a peek into the future for a wide variety of reasons, and people have been looking for ways to do this since time began. There are various methods of divination, and one of them is scrying. The word is loosely defined in most references as a method of foretelling the future by looking into a reflective or transparent surface. This reflective surface can be anything from a crystal or glass ball to a bowl of water or a mirror.

Seer stones are commonly made from clear quartz because it is hard and durable, easy to get hold of, beautiful, and not outrageously expensive. The spherical shape of a seer stone resembles the moon and the womb, harnessing female energy and power. It represents wholeness, infinite potential, the world, and the number zero; the symbol for complete emptiness. It is the shape that can hold the largest amount of any substance within the smallest surface area and it is a three-dimensional symbol of infinity and eternity—it has no beginning and no end.

It was believed that the crystal contained a spirit or an angel, but in fact, it is merely a tool to focus your mind. The multitude of facets and flaws inside the stone reflect millions of tiny points of light that catch and hold your gaze. If you keep staring at the crystal without adjusting your vision, the optic nerve becomes fatigued and stops transmitting the impressions from the outside. It turns inwards and projects the images in the mind so that it appears that they are in the crystal. This is sometimes called the "inner eye." The reflective surface of water or a mirror will produce the same effect.

It doesn't matter whether you're using a quartz crystal, a bowl of water, or a mirror, the procedure for scrying is the same.

- Do your scrying at a time when you won't be disturbed.
- Place your bowl of water, sphere, or mirror on a table that is covered with a dark cloth, preferably black velvet.
- The room should be in semi-darkness, so dim the lights if you have a dimmer switch, or use a soft light such as a candle or night light. Put the candle out of your line of vision so that the flickering of the flame doesn't distract you.
- Sit in a comfortable position at the table and put your hands down flat on either side of your scrying tool. Make sure that your feet are touching the ground.
- Now, close your eyes, relax, and take three slow, deep, breaths. Ground yourself by imagining that there is a network of roots growing out of your feet into the earth all the way to its core. This is an important step because your mind is going to enter a plane beyond your known existence and you need to keep yourself grounded on this one.

- When you are sure that you are properly 'rooted,' open your eyes, cup your hands around the ball, bowl, or mirror and ask your spirit guide to be with you. If you have a question, now is the time to ask it. If you don't have a question, that is fine. Then it is very likely that what you see will answer a question that you might not even have known you had!

- Stay in your relaxed state, and begin to gaze into the ball, mirror, or bowl. If you're using a mirror, it's best to put it at a slight angle so that your reflection doesn't distract you.

- Try and find a single point in the item in front of you that you can focus on and do not shift your gaze or adjust your focus. Just keep staring at it and keep your mind clear. If it feels as if your eyes want to begin to water, you are staring too intensely. Relax a bit. Try to think of nothing at all. This is not easy, and stray thoughts will come peeking into your mind to see what it's doing. When they do, you can imagine a little broom sweeping them away or any other method that you can use to make them go back to where they came from and leave you alone.

- Most people report that the item that they are looking at begins to dissolve into a mist before they 'see,' so don't be alarmed when this happens. It means that it's working!

- Hold your gaze, but don't try to 'look,' because the moment you do that, you will shift your focus and lose the images that are trying to form. Just stay released, and keep gazing, allowing your "inner eyes" to "see."

- Lots of people get so excited at this point because they realize that it's working that they lose their focus and have to start over. That's okay. You'll get used to it and soon you'll be scrying like a pro.

- Sometimes it starts with sensations or feelings that you experience, so take note of those as they could be an important part of what you're going to 'see.'

- Keep on until you feel that you've had enough. You will find that you are seldom able to scry for longer than about twenty minutes because your eyes and mind become fatigued. Make notes of what you experienced so that you can meditate on it later to gain a deeper understanding of what you felt or saw.

Dowsing

Most people know that dowsing is the art of finding objects and substances that are hidden to the naked eye, but fewer people know that you can also dowse to find answers to your questions. Just like all the other aspects of magick, dowsing is an art that can be learned if you are attuned to the universal energies. The most popular tools used for dowsing are a forked piece of wood, two metal rods, or a pendulum. In some countries, hazel is the preferred wood, and some say that the rods should be made of copper and the pendulum should be made of brass, but it really doesn't matter what your tools are made of as long as they serve their purpose for you. You can make your pendulum with a piece of string and a hexagonal nut, if you wish, as long as it's balanced. As always, remember that the tool is just an instrument that helps you channel the magick that is already in you.

Let's quickly look at how dowsing works, because if you can understand it, you should be able to do it. Some people say that dowsing is a natural talent that only some people have, but that is only true if you believe it and allow it to stop you from trying.

Remember we said that every single thing in the universe vibrates at its own special frequency? And remember how we agreed that thoughts and intentions vibrate at the frequency of the thing that you are thinking of? So, it would make perfect sense then; if you are thinking about water, that you are sending a thought into the universe that vibrates at a similar frequency to that of water.

Now, remember the law of attraction that says all things with similar vibrations are attracted to each other? According to this law, if there is water in the vicinity, and your thought vibration about water is strong enough, the two vibrations will resonate with each other and become like two magnets that are being drawn to each other.

The closer you get to the water, the stronger the vibrations will resonate, and you could even get a physical sensation such as tingling in your fingertips or your hair might feel as if it's standing on end. You have now become a magnetic field and your tool is the 'pointer' that is pointing you towards the source of the vibration you are seeking. A forked branch will "point and pull" you in the direction of the water while rods cross over each other to guide you. A pendulum will do what you trained it to do, and it's this interesting little tool that we are going to learn more about because it's so handy.

While you can't carry a forked branch or metal rods in your pocket, you can take a pendulum everywhere. You can wear it around your neck or keep it in your pocket and pull it out whenever you need it. It is also very versatile, and if it is made of a crystal, it can also be used for healing purposes. A pendulum could potentially become one of your favorite tools, and once you have one and know how to use it, you'll wonder how you ever got by without it.

Using your pendulum

Regardless of whether you have a beautiful crystal pendulum, or whether you've got a traditional brass one, or whether you're using a hexagonal nut, you will have to train it before you can use it so that you can interpret its responses. It is recommended that you participate in the exercises below rather than just reading through them as they will have a lot more value for you that way. Also, by the time you're done, you'll have a trained pendulum and you will have practical knowledge of how to use it. When your pendulum is trained, it is specially tuned to your vibration, so if you keep it on you and you don't allow others to touch it, it can become one of your favorite tools for divination.

For the purpose of the lessons below we will be using the most common positions for the responses. Your pendulum may respond differently to these, and that is quite alright as long as the response is always consistent. You will see what we mean by this in a moment.

Holding your pendulum

- You can use any hand you like. Your arm should be in a comfortable position so that your hand can be steady. You can support your elbow on a table if you like.

- Hold the pendulum by its string or chain between your forefinger and thumb. These two fingers should be pointing downwards and the others curled up and out of the way.

- There should be between two and three inches of chain between your fingers and the pendulum so that it can swing freely.

- Use your other hand to bring the pendulum to a complete standstill.

The search position—where all dowsing begins.

- Relax and focus on the pendulum with the intention of teaching it to 'speak' to you. When you are ready, say to the pendulum "Show me my search position."

- The most likely response will be no response at all! However, for some the pendulum will swing very gently back and forth, while for others it could move in tiny circles. Each pendulum has its own character and will behave in its own manner, so you will have to learn each other's languages.

- If your pendulum moved when you asked your question, bring it to a standstill and ask the question again. If it behaves the same way it did the previous time, that's probably your pendulum's way of saying "I'm ready when you are." If not, keep on until you get the same response at least five times in a row.

The 'yes' response

- Always start in the search position. Find it by setting your intention to start dowsing and saying "Let us begin."

- To find out your pendulum's response for 'yes,' ask it a question where the response has to be a definite 'yes.' A good question to ask, is "Does water make things wet?"

- Wait a while to see if your pendulum responds and shows you its movement for 'yes.' If it doesn't, decide what movement you would like for 'yes' and make it move while you say out loud, "This is yes. This is positive."

- Repeat the exercise until you get the same response to your question five times in a row.

The 'no' response

- To find out the response for 'no,' ask a question to which you know the answer is a definite 'no.' A good one to ask is, "Can a rock float on water?"

The "not sure" response

- This response is for when your line of questioning starts going in the wrong direction; your questions don't make sense, or you've asked a question that can't be answered with 'yes' or 'no.'
- Start the way you always do, but now you say to the pendulum "Show me your response for "not sure."
- Watch for the natural response, or teach the pendulum how to respond by repeating the question and forcing it to make the movement you want in the same manner you taught it 'yes' and 'no.'

Using your pendulum

Practice by asking questions about the things around you. Is this made of wood? Is the sun shining? Is this an animal product? Is that the color blue? Keep practicing until your 'yes' and 'no' responses are consistently correct. Now let's try something new.

We're going to use your pendulum to find something. Ask a friend to hide an item from you in a room of your home—they should not tell you where it is, but let's say it's your hat, and they've hidden it under the couch by the window. The window is directly across from the doorway. You are going to ask questions to find out where it is.

Stand in the center of the room facing the doorway. Ask your pendulum, "Is my hat to the front of me?" The pendulum should respond with 'no.' Stay where you are, and ask, "Is my hat to the left of me?" Again, the pendulum should respond with 'no.' Now ask, "Is my hat behind me?" This time the pendulum should respond with 'yes,' so let's assume that it did. Since the pendulum indicated that your hat is somewhere behind you, turn around and start asking questions about what you see in front of you. Remember that your subconscious takes things very literally and only understands absolutes such as "on top of," "under," "inside," "outside," and so on. It does not understand what "near" and "far" or "close to" means and you should get a "not sure" response if you ask, "Is my hat near the couch?"

Your pendulum can help you find your direction if you are lost; it can help you find your lost property, it can help you with healing, or to find water, and a ton of other things, so, if you are fascinated, take some time out to learn more about this fascinating part of your craft.

Other Forms of Divination

Dowsing and scrying aren't the only forms of divination. Another popular method is cartomancy, or "reading cards," and beautiful tarot and oracle cards are available at most bookstores. Other ways to take a peek into the future are palmistry, reading runes, dream analysis, reading tea leaves, throwing bones, and many more.

A word to the wise

It is not really possible to foretell the future. What you are 'seeing' is the most likely outcome if you continue on your current path. So, if you foresee a positive outcome, keep going in that direction, but if you foresee a negative outcome, use the knowledge that you have to help you make decisions that will change your direction and change your outcome. The power is always in your hands.

Conclusion

Our magical journey is almost at its end, and just like witchcraft has grown and developed over the ages, may it be that you have also grown and developed as you journeyed through this book.

We've taken a look at the meaning of the word 'witch' and come to the conclusion that witches are magical people who are in tune with the energies of the universe, understand how they work, and are able to manipulate them to their advantage to achieve the outcomes they desire. We've agreed that these witches can come from all walks of life and that you don't have to actively practice witchcraft to be a witch. We've also seen that we don't need many tools to practice this magical craft, and that nature in its bounty will supply us with all we need if we learn to open our eyes and look.

We also know now why our kind of magick comes with its own special extra letter and what the significance of this is. We've busted some myths about witchcraft and it's been confirmed that no rituals and sacrifices are required and that you don't have to join a coven or belong to any kind of religion to be a witch.

The most important thing we learned about witches is that a witch isn't a 'what,' it's a 'who,' and that that 'who' is a magical individual with special skills that they use to help improve not only their own lives, but also the lives of others. Without even thinking about it, witches also make the world a better place—they are always creating positive vibrations and working to raise their own vibrations to a higher frequency. Because we are all part of the same "pot of soup," raising their vibration, also raises the vibration of the universe.

We've learned that there are seven universal laws that are encompassed by an eighth law—the Law of Attraction. We also know that these are the laws that have governed the universe and all magick since the beginning of time. Until they were described by the physicist, Isaac Newton, these forces were simply seen as supernatural forces that witches had access to and were eyed with either skepticism or superstition.

A stroll through our herb garden taught us about some of the herbs and plants that one can use to make all sorts of lotions, potions, essences, and more. We made a stop in the witch's kitchen where we took a look at the procedures and processes required to produce these products, and then we took a glimpse at their healing properties and how they can be used.

At our next stop, we explored the world of crystals and looked at the properties and uses of these beautiful stones. We only managed to look at a few of the over two hundred stones that can be found around the world when we got distracted by the sweet aroma coming from the shelf where the essential oils are kept. Once again, we could barely touch on the subject before we had to move on to knives, wands, and other tools.

"Hocus Pocus! Ala Kazam!" We know that these words don't work, but they're lots of fun to say anyway. 'Spelling' is one of the most fascinating aspects of witchcraft because there's so much mystery surrounding it. We took a peek under the witch's hat and discovered more about how our understanding of the Law of Attraction and the other universal laws can be used to make our spells effective. We also learned the architecture of spells and how to create our own spells.

The final stretch of our journey took us into the mysterious world "beyond the veil" where we explored our psychic abilities. If you did the dowsing and scrying exercises, it is likely that you experienced a feeling of wonder when you succeeded at it. Maybe you stood in awe for a moment when you understood how your connection to the collective consciousness really works.

A final word

It isn't possible to cover even the basics of modern magick in a little book such as this one, and it was hard to decide what to put in and what to leave out. You may have noticed that, while healing is often mentioned, there is no specific chapter dedicated to this part of the craft. That is because this is a guide for beginners, and healing is for advanced witches and natural healers who instinctively know what to do. There are many kinds of healers, from energy healers, to crystal healers, to Reiki masters, to shamans, to medicine men; all witches, and each with their own way of thinking and doing. If you're a natural healer, you will instinctively know what to do with the information in this book, and hopefully it will point you in the direction that you wish to go.

"*Whatever you fight, you strengthen, and what you resist, persists.*" These words by Ekhard Tolle in his book, A New Earth, remind us to focus on what we want to come to us, and not what we want to go away. The harder you resist something, the more energy you feed it, the stronger it becomes; but when you focus on the positive, on the things that enrich and make your life beautiful, you will draw all of that into your life. You are a wonderful, magical, esoteric being, and the power that is in you is a gift that you can use, not only to make your own life better, but also, to help make the world a better place.

The purpose of this book is not to convince you that you should practice witchcraft, or that you're a witch. Its purpose is simply to introduce you to the intriguing world of magick where not everyone dares to go. It is to tickle your fancy and awaken your interest and dare you and challenge you to explore a deeper and more interesting world than what we see on the surface. It hopes to encourage, and even challenge you to look within to discover your own inner magic so that you can be empowered and free.

May you discover your power. May you use it with love. May you grow in knowledge and wisdom. May you manifest your desires and may you raise the vibration of the Universal Mind with good thoughts and kindness. May the best of your dreams come true. As above, so below; as below, so above. Blessed be.

References

All images were retrieved from pixabay.com and unsplash.com.

Ann-Marie Gallagher. (2003). *The spells bible : the definitive guide to charms and enchantments*. Walking Stick Press.

Buckland, R. (2004). *Buckland's complete book of witchcraft*. Llewellyn Publications.

Cabot, L. (2020). *Laurie Cabot | Understanding Witchcraft*. Fashion-Stylist. https://www.lauriecabot.com/understanding-witchcraft

Cambridge Dictionary. (2019, October 23). *WITCHCRAFT | meaning in the Cambridge English Dictionary*. Cambridge.Org. https://dictionary.cambridge.org/dictionary/english/witchcraft

Cunningham, S., & Nightingale, K. (2017). *Wicca : a guide for the solitary practitioner*. Llewellyn Publications.

Gilbert, R. A. (2020). *Sorcery | occult practice*. Encyclopedia Britannica. https://www.britannica.com/topic/sorcery

Hall, J. (2009a). *The crystal bible : featuring over 200 additional healing stones. Vol. 2*. Godsfield.

Hall, J. (2009b). *The definitive guide to over 200 crystals. v. 1*. Godsfield Press Ltd.

Justis, A. (2016, September 14). *How to Make an Herbal Decoction.* Herbal Academy. https://theherbalacademy.com/herbal-decoction/

Kotsos, T. (n.d.). *The Universal Mind - There is But One Consciousness.* Www.Mind-Your-Reality.Com. Retrieved August 14, 2020, from https://www.mind-your-reality.com/universal_mind.html

Lonegren, S. (2004). *The Pendulum Book* (4th ed.). Connections Book Publishing Limited. (Original work published 1992)

Purkiss, D. (n.d.). *Witchcraft: Eight Myths and Misconceptions.* English Heritage. Retrieved August 14, 2020, from https://www.english-heritage.org.uk/learn/histories/eight-witchcraft-myths/

RachelAndorfer. (2018, November 29). *A Beginner's Guide to Essential Oils Part 1: Essential Oil Extraction.* Tisserand Institute. https://tisserandinstitute.org/beginners-guide-essential-oils-part-1-essential-oil-extraction/

Rihiimaki, L. (2019, February 11). *What Does it Mean to be a Modern Witch?* Gaia. https://www.gaia.com/article/what-does-it-mean-to-be-a-witch

Rose, E. (2012). *MIM - Understanding the Word "Witch" and How it is Used Today.* Sites.Google.Com. https://www.moonlightmessages.com/wicca-101/understanding-the-word-witch

Sake, F. P. (2017, August 3). *Magic vs. Magick vs. Majick.* For Puck's Sake. https://www.patheos.com/blogs/matauryn/2017/08/03/magic-vs-magick-vs-majick/

Sophie Saint Thomas. (2018, April 5). *A Real-Life Witch Debunks 9 Common Myths About Witchcraft*. Allure; Allure. https://www.allure.com/story/real-life-witches-myths-misconceptions

Taylor, J. (2009). *Crystal Power - Develop your ability to see the future.* Connections Book Publishing Limited.

West, H. (2019, September 30). *What Are Essential Oils, and Do They Work?* Healthline; Healthline Media. https://www.healthline.com/nutrition/what-are-essential-oils#how-they-work

Wright, M. S. (2020, July 9). *Five Spell-Casting Essentials for Beginner Witches*. Exemplore. https://exemplore.com/wicca-witchcraft/Witchcraft-For-Beginners-The-Five-Essential-Parts-of-Casting-Spells

www.ingramcontent.com/pod-product-compliance
Ingram Content Group UK Ltd.
Pitfield, Milton Keynes, MK11 3LW, UK
UKHW022017190726
13853UKWH00005B/1977